THE CONNOISSEUR NEW GUIDES

English Painting and Sculpture

Tudor – Early Victorian

Adonis Departing for the Chase by J. M. W. Turner.
By courtesy of the Gallery of Modern Art, New York.

THE CONNOISSEUR NEW GUIDE TO

English

PAINTING AND

SCULPTURE

TUDOR – EARLY VICTORIAN

Edited by L. G. G. Ramsey, Editor of *The Connoisseur*

With an Introduction by Edward Lucie-Smith

THE CONNOISSEUR LONDON

The Connoisseur New Guides
have been adapted from articles in
The Connoisseur Period Guides
(edited by Ralph Edwards and L. G. G. Ramsey)

Designed and produced for *The Connoisseur*
by George Rainbird Ltd, 11 Charlotte Street, London W1,
and printed by Richard Clay and Company Ltd,
The Chaucer Press, Bungay, Suffolk

© The Connoisseur 1962

Contents

Introduction

VARIOUS attempts have been made to define the essential "Englishness" of English art, including Professor Pevsner's in a memorable series of Reith Lectures. The revealing thing is that they should have been considered necessary. As a phenomenon, English art is apt to induce a profound uneasiness in its historians. The English national school is the most paradoxical and difficult to grasp of all the great European schools of painting and sculpture. Its progress sometimes appears fitful, its great talents ambiguous and hard to evaluate correctly.

This book performs a great service by relating English painting and sculpture so firmly to their social background. Without an understanding of English patrons, their tastes, their prejudices, their background, their particular attitudes to art and artists at various stages in our history, we can never hope to attain any understanding of the painters and sculptors who worked for them.

English patronage of the arts is an astonishing spectacle. In some ways it has always been ruthlessly down-to-earth. For example, English pride of birth and race, combined with English interest in human character, has led to the constant emphasis on portraiture which is discussed in every chapter of this book. Similarly, English feeling for sport led to the development of a whole school of painters (including one genius) whose work is hardly to be paralleled elsewhere. Yet many of the very greatest English artists were gifted with an amazing fantasy – one has only to think of Turner and of Blake.

Two things, however, seem to be constant. One is the intimate link which exists in England between painting and literature. We find it as much in the allegories and mottoes of Tudor portraits, as in Victorian illustrations to *The Deserted Village*. And it is interesting to note that certain English artists, such as Blake and Rossetti, also take a high place as writers.

The other factor is stranger, and has been much less discussed. One finds in English painting a reluctance to drive inwards into the picture-space, which sometimes, especially when the artist is struggling with influences from abroad, leads to a characteristic formal incoherence. Though English collectors deeply appreciated their works (to the extent that many of the most important are still to be found in England), the British have perhaps never produced an artist equivalent to Poussin or to Annibale Carracci. Ideas of weight, mass, volume, of limited and logical space, of solemn plasticity, have never been dominant. It is significant, for example, that Stubbs, whom I take to be the most truly classical in spirit of English painters, exceeding even Wilson in this respect, worked by means of carefully composed arabesques, not by an arrangement of volumes in imagined space.

It is equally significant that two of the most distinguished foreign painters to have worked in England, Hans Holbein and Anthony Van Dyck, should have developed in the same direction – towards the flat, decorative, patterned image, and away from the rendering of volume. This development is particularly strange in the case of Van Dyck, and does much to explain both the fascination and the unevenness of the work he did in England. Van Dyck comes from the central tradition of the Baroque. A look at the portraits of his Genoese and Flemish periods will show what a master he was of Baroque thrust and counterthrust, how often his figures are composed in twisting spirals which define the space they occupy, the mass of air which they displace with their physical presence. But in England that physical presence attenuates, and becomes etherialized. Sometimes, as in the famous portrait of Northumberland, the design is much more a pattern made up of sweeping curves than something convincingly created in three dimensions.

And it is perhaps for this reason, a lack of feeling for plasticity, that English sculpture remained, throughout the period covered by this book, in a secondary role: indeed, it was very largely in the hands of foreign artists. Flaxman, one of the best of native-born sculptors, was a master of low relief, not of the free-standing figure.

Within the history of English art there is a division. On one side there are the artists who are marked by an outgoing curiosity, a feeling for human beings as they exist in society, which has rarely been equalled abroad. On the other there are those who look not outward to their fellow beings but inward to themselves. The two central figures in the first group are Hogarth and Reynolds. Reynolds, the greater artist of the two, is perhaps still the most underestimated painter England has produced. Partly, this is because his talent was so intensely contradictory. An advocate of the Academic tradition, he hardly fits into it at all comfortably himself. His most striking virtues are his wonderfully subtle *matière*, and his tremendous penetration of human personality. His striking faults are precisely those which we would not expect in an admirer of the seventeenth-century Italians – an uncertainty of contour and of articulation. It is, in short, essential to turn to his drawings in order to understand Reynolds. This in spite of the fact that he is generally supposed to have drawn very little. He *did* draw (though his reasonably numerous sketches tend to survive in unexpected places). And the great thing about many of his drawings is their tremendously calligraphic quality, full of loops and pothooks which seem taken straight from a book by some writing-master. The drawing of *Comedy*, in the Ashmolean Museum, is characteristic. It is not "great draughtsmanship" in the conventional sense, yet it forms an unexpected bridge between Guercino (whom it faintly resembles) and Delacroix (whom it resembles very closely indeed). Reynolds is a romantic before Romanticism. This is why he is able to present character heroically and lyrically, as something universal, as well as something laboriously compiled from particular details of feature and expression.

8

This lyrical quality is something which appears again and again in the best English painting. One sees it in Constable's use of paint as much as Hogarth's. One sees it, too, in the ravishing "innocence" of the early Gainsborough, which Mr Hugh Honour comments on in his chapter devoted to Early Georgian painting.

It is, however, to be found most clearly of all in those "inward-looking" English painters. Blake is an artist of this kind, and so is Palmer. But the artist whom I take to be the greatest of the group, and indeed to be one of the very greatest that Europe has produced since the Renaissance, is J. M. W. Turner. It often seems that Turner is a painter more praised than enjoyed. And indeed he does have very disturbing things about him. But only some of these are truly defects. He has, for example, a tiresome streak of vulgarity. This comes out in competitiveness, in a desire to rival the great dead, such as Claude and the Van de Veldes. His exercises in the manner of other artists are brilliant, but also a trifle high-pitched and strident. There is, in fact, something forced about them. And Turner's literariness can be of the lowest as well as the highest order. There is a certain sort of Turner which is uncomfortably close to "Mad" Martin, and which is only rescued from intolerable rhetoric by the magical sensitivity with which the actual medium is used.

The other things which may be found a little disturbing about Turner ought to be counted amongst his greatest virtues. He is a tremendously prophetic artist. In his late work, he does things which modern painting is only just beginning to do. Not only did he foreshadow the Abstract Expressionists, he also foreshadows, in some pictures, an artist like Francis Bacon. A figure-painting such as *The Letter* in the Tate Gallery only now begins to take on its full stature; with its extraordinary truncations of drawing, its peculiarly expressive distortions, the way in which some things trail off into the surrounding atmosphere, some are sharply realized, yet others (such as the woman's raised arm) deliberately made ambiguous. It is the method adopted by many of the young painters of today who are currently returning to figuration after an experience of abstraction. Scarcely less extraordinary are the sketches at the Tate of *A Skeleton Falling from a Horse* and *Sunrise with a Sea Monster*. These go far beyond conventional Romanticism. They are visionary in a way which is peculiarly English, and which ought to be recognised as probably the greatest merit of the British national school.

One of the most interesting things about Turner is the comparison which can be made between him and certain artists of China and Japan. In some of his Venetian scenes Turner uses an interrupting scarf of mist to give a feeling of boundlessness in just the same way as we see it used in the famous pair of screens depicting pine trees by the sixteenth-century Japanese artist Tohaku which are now in the National Museum, Tokyo.

As is well-known, painting in the Orient can be considered a branch of writing, or writing as a branch of painting. I would like to suggest that this is also true with the work of British artists; though not in so narrowly technical a way. Most people would admit that for William Blake writing and painting were almost interchangeable activities. There is a sense in which this is true of a great deal of English art, where the boundary between literature and the plastic arts is not nearly so firmly fixed as it is elsewhere in Europe. Is this one of the keys to English national sensibility? The idea that English art is "written" as much as painted or carved or drawn or moulded helps to explain many things in its development. Not all is poetry. Much is highly serviceable prose, and a little is empty rhetoric. As this book shows, its expression has varied fascinatingly, not only as English society and English customs have varied, but in accordance with the European spirit of the age.

Edward Lucie-Smith

TUDOR

PAINTING

DAVID PIPER

WHEN, after the Reformation, images were forbidden in English churches, English painting lost not only its subject-matter, but its market and its patron, and whole crafts almost withered within a generation from lack of support, including those of wall-painting and glass-painting. The painters, however, were not yet concerned with the dignity of art, and all of them, from Holbein downwards, would turn their hand to any kind of painting – settings for pageants and masques, decoration of barges and coaches, wall-decoration and even no doubt straightforward house-painting. Much of the painting throughout the Tudor period was ephemeral in nature, and some of their most brilliant *tours de force* must have had a life-span of only a few days, such as the fabulous decorations for the Field of Cloth of Gold. The prospects for more durable and more profound works of art, early in the six-teenth century, were not good; there was no constellation of princely Maecenases to offer patronage, as there was in Italy; there was no established tradition of domestic magnificence in which pictures were acknowledged and eagerly sought after as desirable house furniture. In the great houses of the land, wall-decoration was generally of tapestry, for which a form of painted or stained cloth might serve as cheaper substitute; in lesser houses there was often no decoration at all, and certainly no pictures. Wall-painting, perhaps more common than the surviving fragments might suggest, was mostly purely decorative, tending to patterns like wall-papers. But there are exceptions, such as those from Carpenters' Hall, showing carpenters at work. Occasional mythological or biblical subjects survive elsewhere. It took all the sixteenth century to accustom even the top strata of English society to the habit of hanging paintings on their walls. Their value as decoration is questionable; in the first half of the century, at least, many pictures were provided with a curtain, which was drawn, presumably, only when they were specifically to be looked at. (There may be here a suspicion of the primitive fear of the magic of images; the object may have been to protect the pictures, but was perhaps also to preserve the owners from the images.) Even when the habit was more or less established it was confined mainly to one kind of picture: portraits. The English were accustomed to the idea of tomb-effigies, and much of Tudor portraiture conveys an impression as of effigies domesticated.

Paintings other than portraits. The demand for religious paintings, of course, ceased with the Reformation, and there is little evidence that there was any sudden efflorescence of them in the brief Catholic dominance of Mary I in the 'fifties. There are, however, some sporadic examples later in the sixteenth century of a curious religious-allegorical manner, of which a good specimen is reproduced (Pl. 4A) – a kind of visual tract. There seems again to have been a slight demand for mythological and to a greater extent for allegorical pictures. Professor Waterhouse has suggested that the *Ulysses and Penelope* of 1570 at Hardwick was painted in England, and mythological themes were a primary inspiration of painted hangings and tapestries. Allegory, however, was probably more popular for pictures, and was even amalgamated with portraiture by one considerable artist, Hans Eworth, in pictures produced between 1550 and 1570. It certainly seems likely that a number of allegorical pieces in the Flemish Mannerist style, showing naked gods and goddesses with long and strangely arranged limbs, may have been painted in England by immigrant artists. In the last quarter of the century the allegorical method became extremely rarified, and will be discussed in the section dealing with the problems of Queen Elizabeth's portraits. Of true landscape painting there is hardly a sign in the Tudor period. There are some topographical views of royal palaces, drawings made by the Fleming A. van den Wyngaerde on a flying visit about 1557, and the famous drawing of Nonsuch Palace by Hoefnagel, who was in England about 1568. The same artist's painting of the *Wedding at Horsleydown in Bermondsey* at Hatfield is almost the only genre painting in England of the century, though others are hinted at in inventories, such as the Earl of Leicester's *A Butcher and Maid buying Meat*, by Hubbard. Instead of landscapes the Elizabethans had maps; at Lambeth, for example, in 1575 there were listed with the pictures about thirty maps, some framed, including English and European maps, "a greate mappe of the peregrination of Christ", one of the "Land of Promise", and one of America. The world was opening fast.

"Dynastic painting". Another kind of painting may be isolated here, though as a category it melts into that of portraiture. It is the propaganda picture, religious, political or dynastic. Henry VII's consciousness of his position as the founder of a lineage is reflected in the magnificent chapel at Westminster and in his tomb. It is enlarged upon by his son in Holbein's great wall-painting, which hung in the Privy Chamber at Whitehall (no doubt there strategically placed) and showed Henry VII and his Queen, Henry VIII and one of his (Jane Seymour, mother of the heir), and which was so impressive that it was said still to make people shake even at the end of the century (Pl. 1A). This was elaborated further, late in

Henry VIII's reign, in the strange long picture now at Hampton Court, which shows Henry VIII enthroned with one of his Queens (again Jane Seymour, though long dead, as mother of the heir), and the Prince Edward at their side. At each extreme end of the picture, as though first and second reserves, stand the next in line, the Princesses Mary and Elizabeth. This picture was to be brought up to date in a revised edition painted by Eworth about 1570, in which Mary (now with Philip II of Spain) is attended by figures of War and Discord, whilst Queen Elizabeth is led forward towards the centre of the stage by Peace. There were also straightforward anti-Papal paintings, most notably that at Hampton Court. This has been plausibly attributed [1] to Girolamo da Treviso, an Italian who worked for Henry VIII between 1538 and 1544, and it certainly belonged to Edward VI in 1547, when it was described as "the bishop of Rome [i.e. the Pope] and the four Evangelists casting stones upon him". But the most curious document of this kind unites the religious, political and dynastic themes, and is also as it were an icon of iconoclasm. It shows Henry VIII on his death-bed, handing on the Protestant Succession to the already enthroned Edward VI (Pl. 5B). On the right-hand side is the Protector Somerset with the Council of the protectorate, including Cranmer, and in the foreground the Pope, slumped in his seat, mortally sick, whilst two monks flee away. In the top right-hand corner, a domed church, presumably intended for St Peter's, founders in flames, whilst two armed men break up a statue of the Madonna on a column with lances.

Portraiture and the Tudor collectors. The bulk of Tudor painting remaining to us consists straightforwardly of portraiture. Realistic portraiture was known in England through the fifteenth century, if not much before. It was, however, a rarity, called upon mainly for specific occasions, generally either memorial or marital. Portraits were exchanged between royal houses during marriage negotiations, so that each side might see what the bargain looked like; and probably about the end of the century there seems to have become standardized a set of portraits of the kings of England. Portraits of a lesser rank than royal remain extremely scarce until after 1525, and it was only in Elizabeth's reign that it seems to have become customary for the heads of the most distinguished houses to have themselves recorded in paint. They put themselves on record in these portraits in much the same spirit as they built themselves their splendid tombs, standing in the full pride of their office and their blood, often, for the greater precision, showing their coat-of-arms.

To begin with, paintings had probably no place in less than royal Tudor homes. The little information so far to hand suggests that the earliest private collectors of importance were amongst that group of humanists centred round Sir Thomas More. More himself had other paintings than the "fine painted cloth with nine

[1] By P. Pouncey, *Burlington Magazine*, XCV (1953), pp. 208-10.

pageants and verses" which he had designed himself when a youth for his father, and the Holbein family group. The royal collection is revealed as rich in quantity by inventories of 1542 and 1547, but the quality (apart chiefly from the Holbeins, and the Raphael of St George now in Washington) is difficult to assess, as so few of the pictures are now identifiable. There were, however, besides portraits, a high proportion of religious paintings. Clearly, the Protestant iconoclasm did not extend to private collections, although few new religious pictures were painted in England. The pictures seem to have been distributed through the royal palaces; the main concentrations being probably in the Long Galleries (at Greenwich there was even "In the Jakes house a picture"). But the great characteristic Elizabethan collections did not begin really to accumulate until the 'sixties. At that time the hoards of the Fitzallens, Earls of Arundel, of the Cecils, of Matthew Parker at Lambeth began to swell, but the largest were probably those of Leicester and of the heir of the Arundels, John, Lord Lumley. They were not truly art collections, but specifically portrait collections. In Bess of Hardwick's collection in 1601 there were about seventy portraits (thirty-seven of them in the Long Gallery), as against less than ten other pictures. Leicester, in 1583, had at Kenilworth alone thirty-seven portraits, as against three subject pictures (excluding twenty-three maps and "five of the seven planets painted in frames"). Lumley, about 1600, had some two hundred portraits, but only about thirty other paintings. The portraits were of relations, friends and colleagues, the kings of England and sometimes of Scotland, contemporary celebrities both English and European, irrespective, to a remarkable degree, of political or religious sympathies (both Pole and Cranmer were represented at Lambeth). At Lumley Castle the subjects listed as portraits swept grandly from Adam and Eve onwards, including Julius Caesar, not only Petrarch, but Dante, Raphael, Jane Shore, a complete set of Lumley's own ancestors made up to order, and "old Tyme". Many of these were naturally copies (the extent to which portraits of famous men were copied in the late sixteenth century is one of the factors that makes attributions so difficult a problem). The collections were of celebrities rather than of works of art, but, although the great collectors of the next century, such as Arundel and Charles I, were to winnow taste drastically, the predominant emphasis of English collections upon portraiture thereafter remained constant.

Early portraiture. It is time to consider in more detail the artists who worked in England during this period. The sets of portraits of kings of England (as in the Society of Antiquaries of London) may represent a largely English style. They show (the earliest ones were much copied and revised through the sixteenth century) rather humble, less than life-size figures, half-length, in arched frames of black and gold like niches; the effect being somewhat of a line-and-wash drawing, delicate, linear, attenuated, a little pale and reserved in characterization. The style

survives until well into the century, and a similar pallor and reserve will be characteristic of the Elizabethan portraits. One of the best early specimens is the portrait
of the Countess of Salisbury of about 1530–5, now in the National Portrait Gallery
(Pl. 1B). Here too is a portrait of Henry VII, dated 1505, probably by Michel
Sittow, an international court-painter; it is a stronger and much more vivid affair,
though in the same tradition, representing the corresponding style current in
North European courts. It can have had little effect in England, as it went abroad
immediately, as part of a marriage bid for one of Maximilian's daughters. A different, though by no means novel, concept of portraiture is shown in the painting
of the English merchant Withypol, at Bristol, by Antonio da Solario, 1514 (Pl.
4B). It now seems very possible that this Venetian painter visited England in the
second decade of the century. This is a "donor" portrait, showing the sitter in
adoration before the Virgin, and is part of a triptych, destined probably as altar-
piece for a church or chapel. Doubtless other similar paintings were commissioned,
including portraits, but, being in churches, they almost all would have fallen vic-
tims to the Protestant iconoclasts later in the century.

The sixteenth century is liberally supplied with artists' names, culled from docu-
mentary records, but very meagerly supplied with paintings that can be attached
with any certainty to those names.[2] Thus, in the first half of the century, we know
that there was a considerable influx of Italian talent: the Neapolitan artist Volpe,
in England between 1513 and 1536; Antonio Toto, here between about 1519 and
1555, and Serjeant-Painter; Nicholas da Modena, a considerable artist, here between 1537 and 1568; and the already mentioned Girolamo da Treviso, who arrived about 1542, and was killed in Henry VIII's service at the siege of Boulogne,
1544. There were others, but hardly anything of consideration in the way of paintings can be ascribed to any of them. In the same period, we know the names of
English painters such as John Brown and Andrew Wright, Serjeant-Painters between 1512 and 1532 and 1532 and 1543: yet not a line of their work is known.
There were also active in England between the 'twenties and 'forties various members of the Ghent family of painters, the Horenbouts, and of one Fleming (?),
Joannes Corvus, we have two reasonably certain works, one of Bishop Foxe,
rather stronger and more sculptural in quality than the English manner.

Holbein. The only artistic personality who emerges from the early sixteenth-
century mists, amongst the painters, is Hans Holbein (1497/8–1543); but he with
such stunning clarity that the work of all other painters in England throughout the
century pales in contrast like ghosts. Holbein arrived in late 1526 (withdrawing
from Bâle as a result of the drying-up there of patronage following upon the Protestant triumph). He was already a formed and mature artist, aware of the work of

[2] The archival material for the whole period is very fully summarized by Dr E. Auerbach, *Tudor Artists*,
1954. The best general account of sixteenth century painting is in E. K. Waterhouse, *Painting in Britain,
1530–1790*, 1953.

Raphael and of da Vinci, and he came bearing an impeccable passport from the great Erasmus to Thomas More. Within More's own circle, he was welcomed, and employed, and there he painted not only a number of individual portraits of the first order – including More himself, Archbishop Warham and Tuke – but his masterpiece, the More family group, which is now known only from copies. This, though it inspired no immediate fashion, was the first of English conversation pieces. Holbein's clientèle did not spread much wider, and he returned to Bâle early in 1528. Only on his second visit, from 1532 onwards, did he achieve real Court patronage. Henry VIII seems to have first sat to him about 1536, and there-after Holbein, in the brief seven years left to him (he died of the plague in 1543), painted courtiers, was sent abroad to take likenesses of prospective royal brides (*The Duchess of Milan* in the National Gallery, and the *Anne of Cleves* in the Louvre) and produced the definitive account in paint of Henry VIII himself, in-cluding the great dynastic piece of Henry VIII, Henry VII, Elizabeth of York and Jane Seymour. He also made prolific designs for objects which ranged from jewellery to chimney-pieces. Another source of employment was the German com-munity in London, particularly the Hanseatic merchants of the Steelyard, for whom he painted not only portraits but two large allegories: the *Triumph of Poverty* and the *Triumph of Riches*, now known only from copies.

The quality in Holbein's work that must most have intrigued the English was its naturalism – illusionism. No painter in England before had possessed anything approaching this power to summon up, in a flat, two-dimensional image, the solid weight and living presence of a sitter. This depended equally on his fabulous skill and on the pictorial genius that could combine such acute recording of detail with an infallible grasp of plastic form and design. His sitters sat to him but briefly: as a rule probably only once, long enough for him to take a drawing of their heads (Pl. 2A) – possibly with the aid of some mechanical device of the nature of a *camera obscura*. The portraits of his first English period (Pl. 6B) have a truly humane breadth and grandeur, fully consonant with the character of his chief patron, Sir Thomas More. In the second English period a more hieratic conception pervades, especially in his royal portraits, the figure being sometimes almost as if cut out against the empyrean background, at once glossy and marmoreal in their stiff grandness. With this goes an increased emphasis on surface texture and on the flat patterning of design. This trend foreshadowed the development of English sixteenth-century portraiture and carried to its logical extreme in the late portraits of Elizabeth.

The generation after Holbein. Scholars continue to be baffled by the problem of Holbein's studio. He must have had some extremely able assistants, yet none of them has so far been identified, and there is little work dating from immediately after his death that can be associated plausibly with them. A painter called John Bettes, by whom one portrait is known (Tate Gallery), is clearly very dependent on Holbein's style. Other painters of whom a little is known are all foreign, and fundamentally closer in style to continental trends than to Holbein, though they are not entirely free of his influence. Gerlach Flicke, a German, worked in England from 1547 or before until his death in 1558; Guillim Scrots, or Stretes, a Netherlander with experience of court-portraiture with Mary of Hungary, was here from about 1545 to 1553; the work associated with Hans Eworth, from Antwerp, ranges from 1549 or before until about 1574. Flicke, as his portrait of Archbishop Cranmer shows (Pl. 3c), rivals Holbein in the bold clarity of his characterization, but is more brutal and blatant and far inferior in subtlety, close in mood and composition to painters of the Westphalian school. In a whole-length of Edward VI attributed to Scrots (Pl. 6A), there is a more refined blend of Holbein and of continental influences – the young King's pose is clearly based on that used by Holbein for Henry VIII, though more elegantly mannered. Very similar designs were used throughout Europe during the rest of the century for official royal portraits. Other portraits of Edward VI and of the Princess Elizabeth, of a less rigid but equally accomplished quality, are at Windsor. They are three-quarter-lengths and both are by unidentified artists. In Queen Mary's reign, at the time of her marriage with Philip II of Spain, Antonio Mor came over for a brief visit. No certain portraits, other than that of Mary (Pl. 3A), were painted in England by him, but later English portraiture has more in common with the continental style, of which Mor was the most accomplished exponent, than with Holbein. The characteristic formula, derived in part from designs by Titian, but cooler, the colour smoothly glazed, was a three-quarter-length – the sitter at once more polite, more detached, than with Holbein, and with a narrower design and character in contrast to his generally broad confrontation.

"Hans Eworth". The most interesting and various work of the period is signed in various forms of a monogram: HE. This is generally associated with a Flemish painter from Antwerp called Hans Eworth, but the work generally given as his may be by two or more distinct hands. The earliest known monogrammed works of HE, of 1549 and 1550, are entirely novel to English art: the exotic small-scale painting of a Turk on horseback (Pl. 2B), and the two portraits of Sir John Luttrell and of Captain Wyndham. The Luttrell portrait is a curious composite of mannerist allegory and realistic portraiture, showing the sitter wading naked in a stormy sea, whilst a very classicized goddess leans to him from a cloudy heaven above. The whole picture is, in addition, liberally scattered with inscriptions and mottoes. The Wyndham portrait (Pl. 2C), on the other hand, is the first truly informal portrait in England, showing a soldier as though in a lull in battle, with

B

gun and powder flask, leaning against a tree – burly, untidied, almost sweaty. But these three very different paintings do not seem to have caught on, and by 1554 HE was working for the Court. His portrait of Mary I is a very formal (though successfully so) regal document, reminiscent of Holbein's *Duchess of Milan*, but with an impersonal emphasis on pattern and that cool aloofness that hints at Mor. HE's portraits of the later 'fifties and 'sixties all show a rich incrustation of detailed magnificence in costume, coupled with a curious inflated rotundity of flesh, the figures sharply lit and detached against the background; there seems to be a progressive flattening of the overall pattern, and, in the twin portraits of the Duke and Duchess of Norfolk, 1562 (Pl. 5A), the main elements of the late Elizabethan portrait are already visible. About 1569, we find HE reverting to mannerist mixtures, but now in the special and apt case of Queen Elizabeth herself, for whom a simultaneous presentation in terms both mortal and divine was fitting. One example is the Tudor family piece (described on page 13), and the other is the well-known painting at Hampton Court, also a revision, this time of the Judgement of Paris story. The Queen has usurped the rôle of Paris, having awarded to herself the apple or orb as the most beautiful of them all, whilst the three claimant goddesses are routed in disordered acknowledgement of their better.

From the 'sixties and 'seventies, there survives a number of formal three-quarter-length portraits by unknown artists, monotonous in composition and rarely inspiring in quality. One known artist who painted such portraits was Steven van der Meulen, from Antwerp, naturalized in England in 1562; the *John, Lord Lumley* (1563), still at Lumley Castle, is certainly by him, and a considerable number of other portraits are very close in manner, though doubtless the work of several different artists. Typical examples, though of varying quality, are the *Leicester*, and the *Sir William Petre* of 1567, both in the National Portrait Gallery, and the portraits of Burghley and his wife at Hatfield, the last two verging on the style of Hans Eworth. They are dignified, but rather tame and anonymous in handling, and represent a Court style that was international. Steven van der Meulen had painted also at the Court of Sweden, whilst the portrait of Sir Nicholas Throckmorton in the National Portrait Gallery, which dates probably from 1562 (another version is so dated), in which year Throckmorton was mainly in France, is very reminiscent of Clouet's portrait of Pierre Quthe of the same date in the Louvre. The Throckmorton may, however, have been painted either in England or in France. Rather later, the portrait of Sir Philip Sidney, 1577, seems perfectly consonant with English work, but was probably originated in the Low Countries. Less than life-size portraits, similarly posed, also remained popular. One unnamed painter, by whom several portraits are known, is the artist of the fiercely doll-like Hugh Fitzwilliam. Whole-length portraits, such as *The Earl of Pembroke* on loan from the Duke of Leeds to Lancaster House, are relatively rare, and generally follow in composition and atmosphere the example of Scrots' *Edward VI*.

The Portraits of Queen Elizabeth. In the 'seventies, the portraiture of Queen Elizabeth began to present its own specialized problem: that of reconciling the not entirely pristine appearance of an ageing woman with the concept of ideal, fadeless and beautiful majesty that she represented. Already, by 1563, her portraits were the cause of some concern, and action was meditated along the lines of standardizing a pattern portrait by some "special cunning painter", whence satisfactory and inoffensive copies might be reduplicated. There was clearly a large demand for her portrait, and it was probably the first painting to hang in many English homes. In her famous interview with Nicholas Hilliard (presumably in, or before, 1572) she made clear her own views: especially that to model the figure by light-and-shade was wrong, that it should, on the contrary, be lit by a clear and even light, and scrupulously contoured and delineated – an idea exactly in line with the Italian theorists of Mannerism. It was an idea that, with its apparent insistence on the presentation of the sitter under ruthlessly searching illumination, might seem to make the necessary compromise in her portraits almost impossible. The solution is however latent in a drawing of her (Pl. 3B) made by one of the most eminent of the Italian Mannerist painters, Federigo Zuccaro (who, in spite of the countless portraits ascribed to him in English houses and sale-rooms, was in England for less than a year, in 1574–5; no painting made by him in England is known to exist). The drawing is free and attractive in line – that was to be no part of the solution – but in the background is a column entwined with a snake. Both column and snake are fraught with symbolic significance, and it was to be through allegory and symbolism that Her Majesty was henceforth largely to be demonstrated in her portraits rather than by any accurate reflection of her physical presence. We find her withdrawn behind the richly jewelled and embroidered fabric of her incredible wardrobe: the red wig, the confection of lace, the bolstered sleeves, the iron V of the bodice planted in the great circular hoop of the skirt, the jewellery, the rigging of pearls (themselves symbols). Her face is represented by a summarized and expressionless mask, unwrinkled and ageless. Stiffly she stands, an all but religious image, for veneration. On and about her are the attributes of her majesty – branches of olives, the sheathed sword, the crown, the claimed globe itself; jewels representing a phoenix or a pelican in its piety; or a map of England beneath her feet, thunderous storm and sunshine to left and right, or a whole rainbow clasped bodily in the hand; and, amongst it all, mottoes, even whole sonnets.

Late Elizabethan painters. This richness of emblematic lore is not entirely confined to Elizabeth's own portraits: it is indeed an essential idiom of Elizabethan imagination, and the literature is seamed and studded with it. Hilliard's miniatures are often conceived in that idiom, and it intrudes into and sometimes dominates other life-size portraits. It is symptomatic of a literary rather than a plastic approach to the arts. One may suspect that even the bodies in the portraits may be but emblems for man, or clothes-horses. But the clothes indicate rank and blood: hence, too, perhaps the Elizabethan indifference to visual coherence and to scale – life-size portraits are but blown-up miniatures in conception. Of the painters themselves, we again know as yet very little, but at least some of them, like Hilliard, seem to be native English. George Gower was one. He was well established by 1570 and Serjeant-Painter from 1581 to his death in 1596. The bust portrait of Sir Thomas Kytson (Tate Gallery), 1573, is certainly by him. A few other bust portraits are known, and a fairly certain three-quarter-length is the *Sir Thomas Cornwallis* at Audley End (Pl. 7B). His portraits have something of Hilliard's lucid modesty, but, in the simplified planes of the face, are more sculptural in feeling. Between about 1580 and 1600 we also know a little of Segar – Sir William Segar, also herald and Garter King-at-Arms, and his brother Francis. It may well be that they worked in partnership, and on a miniature as well as life-size scale. *The Earl of Essex*, dated 1590, in Dublin, is a reasonably certain example of Segar's work, and this, though more gauche, is very close to a life-sized exercise in Hilliard's manner. Hilliard himself is known to have worked on a large scale, but no certain example has been discovered and, until one is, his quality on that scale cannot be assessed. There were also active at the time a group of painters mainly of Flemish origin, settled in England: the de Critz and the Gheeraerts families, and, associated with them, an Englishman (?) Robert Peake, and also the miniaturist Isaac Oliver. As de Critzes, Gheeraerts and Olivers inter-married, and the families may have collaborated, some sort of joint studio is possible. At all events their work so far has resisted all attempts at disentanglement. A portrait by John de Critz (c. 1552–1642) is *The Earl of Salisbury* (Hatfield), repeated in many versions, the Earl later re-dressed in Garter robes. Marcus Gheeraerts the younger, who worked probably from the 'eighties until almost 1630, is recorded by various documents and a number of portraits so diverse in manner that the individuality of his style, if any, is far from apparent. The same applies to Robert Peake. The outstanding achievement of the time, however, for part of which this group must have been responsible, is the series of splendidly decorative whole-length portraits produced from the 'eighties for over forty years, until almost 1630. Jointless images, dressed in costumes of great brilliance, posed generally by a gold-fringed velvet chair under a canopy or tent of rich curtains, they are often as flat and almost as formal as the patterned Turkey carpets which most of them feature. The renaissance concepts of depth, of plasticity, of the *vraisemblable*, are here abandoned for an effect almost as though a Byzantine artist had turned his hand to fashion-plates. They are best seen in mass, as at Redlynch Park; there is a good single example in *The Duke of Buckingham* (c. 1616) in the National Portrait Gallery.

The end of the Elizabethan tradition. These whole-lengths constitute a remarkable and uniquely English departure from the mainstream of European painting. The European tradition, however, with its concern for a more naturalistic portraiture, had never been lost from sight in England, and Elizabethan portraiture as a whole steers somewhere between the more naturalistic art of the Netherlands and the extreme stylization of the "Jacobethan" whole-lengths, the high fashion of the Court. A family like the Greshams, wealthy international merchants and financiers, shows an interesting pattern of patronage. Already, in 1544, Sir Thomas Gresham had a whole-length of himself, of remarkable dramatic flamboyance, perhaps painted abroad. In the 'sixties he sat, probably in Flanders, to Mor.

Wood-cut tail-piece from *Caveat or Warneing for . . . Vagabones*, printed by W. Griffith, London 1567.

William Gresham, in 1579, sat like a sober Dutch merchant to the Dutch painter Cornelius Ketel, who was working in England between 1573 and 1581. Some of Ketel's portraits conform to the usual Court designs, but his *Frobisher* of 1577 in the Bodleian Library (Pl. 25A) irrupts, in spite of its damage, into the waxen canon of Court portraiture like a live bandit into Madame Tussaud's. Burly and intransigent, here there is at last more suggestion of movement. Closer to the Anglo-Flemish manner there is the Antwerp painter Hieronymus Custodis, active in England in the 'eighties and dead by 1593, by whom several signed and dated portraits exist. It was the realistic European tradition that was in fact to prevail. The fading of Hilliard before the fleshier talent of Isaac Oliver in the first decade of the seventeenth century is symptomatic of the shifting taste, and in the second decade there arrived from the Low Countries some able and up-to-date painters, including van Somer and Mytens, and the stiff "Jacobethan" formulae began to melt. They were to be liquidated finally only by the arrival of Van Dyck and the Baroque in 1632.

SCULPTURE

ERIC MERCER

By the early years of the sixteenth century English sculpture, despite the skill and training of its practitioners, was barren of ideas. Its motifs were few and hackneyed, and its standard of carving, while still high, was well below the delicate accomplishment of a mid-fifteenth-century work such as Humphrey of Gloucester's chantry at St Albans. Sculptural stonework was largely disappearing from domestic building and the effigies and figures on tombs were becoming competently conventionalized. There was still an occasional liveliness and freshness of approach, as in the Last Judgement on a tomb at Kingston-upon-Soar and the Virgin and Child at Broadwater, both of about 1540, but such qualities were not to survive the Reformation and the advent of patrons who guarded their position in this world only a shade less jealously than their place in the next, and did not intend to have the one or the other compromised by boisterous genre scenes or by idolatrous saints and virgins.

In this situation the arrival of artists like Torrigiani and Giovanni da Maiano, trained in the schools of the Italian Renaissance, had a widespread but not deep effect. Their work in sculpture stands out from that of their English contemporaries as Holbein's does in painting; not merely because they were greater artists, but because of the way in which they were greater. Torrigiani's tomb of Henry VII at Westminster and da Maiano's work at Hampton Court introduced into England a conception of sculptural modelling and of the human figure wholly unknown here before. They also introduced quite incidentally a new set of motifs. English craftsmen borrowed the decorative detail and rejected the essential form of Italian Renaissance sculpture. Before long on tombs, and much less frequently in private houses, renaissance or sub-renaissance details were surrounding wholly un-renaissance English figures. The Marney tomb at Layer Marney (Pl. 11) is an early example, the work of John Guldon of Hereford with its *quattrocento* motifs and its ill-proportioned human figures is a late one. On a domestic building such as Sutton Place of the 1520's, where an attempt was made at introducing renaissance cherubs, the result is merely a series of small naked figures, lively and amusing, but not removed in spirit or execution from late Gothic work.

This failure of an imported sculpture to take root in England occurred again in the third quarter of the century. There is a series of tombs in Buckinghamshire and Bedfordshire distinguished by their severely correct classical detail and their sculptural modelling. The tomb of Sir Robert Dormer at Wing has well-proportioned Corinthian columns supporting a correct entablature and flanking a tomb chest in the shape of a Roman altar with finely carved bucrania and fruit-swags. The monuments of Anthony Cave at Chicheley and of Lord Mordaunt at Turvey are remarkable for their sculptured figures. Although those at Chicheley are, in fact, ill-proportioned, nevertheless they and the admirable figures at Turvey have great elegance and a remarkable freedom of pose. The reclining female figures in the spandrels of Caius' Gate of Virtue at Cambridge, although less well carved, have the same elongated elegance. These examples are of importance not because they had, but because they had not, any influence. They emphasize the lesson of the earlier years, that in essentials English sculpture went its own way in the sixteenth century.

Funeral monuments. The direction of that way was largely determined by the restricted demand for sculpture, a demand that was mainly confined to funeral monuments for the wealthier classes. The best-known native school up to and beyond the middle of the century was that of the Midland alabasterers, but all the work of the period until the very last years of the century is essentially similar. It might use Renaissance or even occasionally Gothic motifs, the effigies might be on an altar tomb or beneath an architectural canopy, the ancillary figures of weepers or children might be standing or kneeling, the standard of execution might vary from the competent work of the Burton alabasterer, Richard Parker, to the crudity of the carver of the Poulet tomb at Hinton St George, but, whatever their foibles or talent, its sculptors had two features in common: they gave their figures a stiffness of pose, and their standing figures a lack of proportion, generally in the direction of squatness, that distinguish them at once from the work of the Italians and from that of the sculptor of the Mordaunt tomb. The stumpy figures on Parker's tomb of the Earl of Rutland at Bottesford (Pl. 8), those on the Royleys' Fermor tomb at Somerton are as ill-proportioned in one way as the lanky figures on the Duchess of Suffolk's tomb at Spilsby or on the Harford tomb at Bosbury are in another. The stiffness of pose resulted mainly from the prevailing attitude towards funeral monuments, the proportions from the designers' failure to solve the problems of relating human figures to classical architecture and from the general unconcern for the human form. In sculpture that was non-monumental but still placed in an architectural framework – the Nine Worthies along the second storey at Montacute, James I and his family at Trinity College, Cambridge, the figures on the chimney-piece at Condover – the pose was very much freer, but the proportions were still squat. Less obviously this unconcern for the human form is revealed in the innumerable thermae of wood and stone in domestic work, figures that were borrowed from abroad, no doubt, but which were seized on with relish because they allowed free play to a delight in facial representation, but set the carver no problem in physical proportions.

Portraiture. It was to the delineation of the human face that the sculpture of the time devoted its greatest skill and care. Although there is no certain proof, the variety of facial types in the alabaster monuments of the period up to 1550 suggests deliberate attempts at portraying individuals. In the later years the London or "Southwark" sculptors were contracting to make the "picture or similitude" of the deceased, and the inscription on the tomb of Sir Robert Watter and his wife at York boasts that their effigies are their "true portraiture". The increasing fashion from about 1580 onwards for bust monuments illustrates the tendency to dispense with the superfluities and provide the essential likeness. On the Suffolk tomb at Spilsby, where the figures are execrable, the busts are at least competent. In the much later tomb of Provost Murray at Eton the bust replaces an effigy as a central feature and is cut and modelled with great skill, whilst the cherubs above it have met with a more cavalier treatment. In those rare instances where sculpture had a domestic setting, as at Lumley Castle, the figures were nearly always busts or half-busts. But at Lumley the one full-length figure, standing upon a fountain, was un-draped, well proportioned and freely posed. The female figure surmounting a fountain that was made for the courtyard at Hampton Court in 1591–2 is similarly well-proportioned and freely posed. These and the statues that were placed in gardens and courtyards, generally of characters from classical mythology, were free of the limitations imposed by an architectural setting or by any intimations of mortality, and gave their sculptors the opportunity, if no more, of breaking the restrictive bounds that hampered the monumental sculptors and their associates.

The London school. In the later years of the century the Anglo-Flemish style of the London sculptors spread widely and either ousted or influenced the provincial craftsmen. Much has been made of this Flemish influence, but it too, like its con-tinental predecessors, was at first mainly confined to detail. The funeral monu-ments were on a larger scale and even more architectural in composition; they were often designed with a great deal of coloured stone and marble in geometrical patterns, and were covered with the conventional motifs of strapwork and of ribbon-scroll; they tended to have coarse mouldings, and especially the heavy belly-mould to horizontal features. In essentials of composition, and consequently in their attitude to the human figure, they differed but little from the native tombs. Yet that little was to be important. One feature which they occasionally introduced was one or more figures of the "Virtues", or other emblematical con-ceptions, placed upon the cornice of the monument and thus unconditioned in their form and volume by any necessity to fit an already determined space. Such figures did not have their proportions determined by non-sculptural considerations, and because they were "emblems" and not mourners, from whom a "modest stillness and humility" in the presence of the mighty dead was demanded, they could be given much freer poses.

The work of these men of the London or "Southwark" school was, however, more a response to, than the origin of, a country-wide demand. The tomb of John Leweston of about 1584 in Sherborne Abbey – a tomb that is clearly not Southwark work or in any way derived from it – has six free-standing cherubs upon its cornice. What the Southwark sculptors did was to follow the age; they turned the provincial cherubs of Sherborne into the fashionable emblematic figures, and then used their superior skill to exploit to the full the new artistic freedom. By the second decade of the seventeenth century the free-standing "Virtues" and all their cousins were a necessary part of every sculptor's stock-in-trade and were being used, however clumsily, by local craftsmen in the remotest parts of England (Pl. 9).

The effigies themselves were not wholly immune from this development. Although the flat-on-the-back attitude never wholly disappeared, it was increasingly superseded by freer poses. The reclining effigy, of which the Hoby tomb at Bisham is a very early example, was soon accompanied by the kneeling effigy, a form which culminated in the seated "Conversation Piece", to use Mrs Esdaile's phrase, of the figures of Sir Giles Mompesson and his wife at Lydiard Tregoze.

With this freedom of pose went, in some cases, a new freedom of emotion that reached its fullest development in the work of Epiphanius Evesham in the early seventeenth century. In place of the professional "weepers" or of stiffly posed and expressionless children of earlier tombs Evesham, as on the monument of Lord Teynham at Lynsted, allowed the dead man's children free and varied poses and a considerable display of grief (Pl. 10). He was not singular in this, and the new emotional content together with the freer poses of the later Southwark School mark the end of the austere and restricted sculpture of sixteenth-century England.

STUART

PAINTING

OLIVER MILLAR

THE age of the Stuarts is a rich and fascinating period in the history of painting in England and the development of English connoisseurship. In its earlier years the number of private collections of any size was limited almost entirely to the Court circle. The motives behind the formation of these collections remained predominantly, as in the previous century, iconographical, historical and dynastic. Pictures had not yet come to be valued as works of art in their own right or as sources of aesthetic delight to their owners, and tapestries or painted hangings were still the accepted form of decoration in a private house. Even in the large and rapidly increasing collection of pictures in the royal palaces there was a preponderance of contemporary and historical portraits, topographical views and maps: Charles I, the most enthusiastic and discerning of all royal patrons and collectors, wholly transformed the Crown collections, but likewise assembled a very large and varied collection of portraits of his family and ancestors, of earlier and contemporary European rulers, of his closest friends and of the artists he admired or who had worked for him. In the other great and lesser collections which grew up in the seventeenth century there was the same continuing interest in the portrait and some patrons even commissioned painters to concoct gratifying sets of "ancestors". The most significant example of an historical portrait gallery was assembled by the Earl of Clarendon at Clarendon House as a commentary on his famous *History*, but something of the flavour of these collections can still be felt at Woburn, where the portraits assembled by the Earls and Dukes of Bedford survive fairly intact; at Welbeck, with its remarkable concentration of likenesses of the Cavendish, Vere, Holles, Harley, Wriothesley and Bentinck families; at Althorp, where a series of portraits of the Spencers and their relatives (a series of consistently high quality) runs from the sixteenth to the twentieth century; at Gorhambury, Drayton, Penshurst, Hardwick, Arbury, Boughton, Belvoir and Knole; at Euston, which still houses the remains of the collection of family and historical portraits formed by the Earl of Arlington; in such Scottish houses as Penicuik, Drumlanrig and Leslie House; and throughout the British Isles, where a steady succession of family portraits forms the backbone of numberless country-house collections.

In the reign of Charles I, and indeed in the last years of his father's reign, there had been a sudden flowering of connoisseurship in the King's immediate circle and an awakened interest in the arts of the Renaissance and contemporary Europe. The Grand Tour had become an increasingly important and regular part of a gentleman's education and some Englishmen had undergone an even deeper experience of European civilization. The structure of patronage, collecting and taste that we associate with the age of Hogarth and Reynolds was already formed in the age of Anne, and there was already a strongly cosmopolitan flavour in the "state of the arts" in the days of the later Stuarts. The great collections of European pictures that were formed in this country in the century after the Peace of Utrecht were anticipated by such travellers and collectors of taste and discernment as the Duke of Shrewsbury, the fifth Earl of Exeter, the second Earl of Sunderland and Sir Thomas Isham: the three last, for instance, had grafted on to their hereditary collections at Burghley, Althorp and Lamport pictures which gave a Mediterranean lustre to their English walls. The same susceptibility to European influences is of fundamental importance for the growth of landscape painting and the lesser genres in England in our period, and an admiration, even in severely Protestant minds, for the full baroque style of Italy, France or Flanders bore fruit in the reflection of continental baroque and early rococo in the work of decorative painters on the walls and ceilings of many English palaces, castles and houses.

Jacobean portraiture still presents a most complex problem. Many portraits were produced in the first two and a half decades of the century and we know the names of painters who were then at work. Within this rather narrow context there is a considerable variety of quality and style and some of the grandest Jacobean pieces are truly impressive. But it is impossible to link the most splendid of them (or, indeed, many of those whose appeal is gentler and less spectacular) with safety to any of the available painters; the slightly more familiar painters, such as Marcus Gheeraerts the younger, John de Critz, Paul van Somer, and even Daniel Mytens in his earlier English period, are still very inadequately defined. The most sumptuous among Jacobean portraits seem to represent a belated and distinctively English form of the mannerist style that was current in the courts of Europe in the sixteenth century. The painters who created them concentrated on an elaborate and often highly polished surface-pattern; the designs are rigid, the figure is often narrow and attenuated; and the decorative value of costume, accessories and setting was thought more important than an attempt to evoke the sitter's personality (see page 20).

In the second decade of the century we can sometimes detect tendencies towards restraint and a more sensitive understanding of the character of the sitter: tendencies that can be guardedly described as English. The pieces in which they are most clearly seen could perhaps be very tentatively associated with John de Critz, Robert Peake or Marcus Gheeraerts: certainly Gheeraerts's portraits of the 1620's have a reserve and simplicity that can be seen in a rather different form in the less attractive work of Paul van Somer, but which are associated particularly with Daniel Mytens and Cornelius Johnson.

Mytens and Johnson were profoundly influenced by contemporary portrait-painting in the fashionable studios of Miereveld and Ravesteyn in Delft and The Hague: Mytens was trained in The Hague and was established in London by 1618, but Johnson, who came of Netherlandish stock, had been born in London, and his portraits have an indefinably English delicacy in mood, close though they are in design to the Dutch school from which both painters derived. The Anglo-Netherlandish style, of which Mytens and Johnson were the main exponents, but which can be seen in the work of such less familiar or more migratory painters as Abraham Blyenberch, Geldorp, Johann Priwitzer or the monogrammist VM, marks a great advance on the flamboyant earlier "Jacobethan" manner: simpler and more worldly, more sensitive in technique and with a feeling for texture which is wholly Dutch. These qualities, and Mytens's grave sense of character, can be seen in his earliest and rather timid English full-lengths (Pl. 12); but in his latest English portraits, the most distinguished that were painted in this country before Van Dyck's arrival, they are enhanced by a new elegance and swagger, manipulated with complete assurance, and enriched by sophisticated colour and broad, free handling.

Cornelius Johnson was a more limited painter and was most at ease with heads and shoulders, often set within the painted oval which he did much to popularize in this country. His earliest pieces, which are usually painted on panel, are tentative and insubstantial, though they have a Jacobean richness of texture; but his style became broader and softer, with a delicacy of colour and touch exactly suited to his tender, perceptive vision (Pl. 13A). He never seems to have worked for as illustrious a clientèle as Van Dyck or Mytens and for some years he was painting portraits for the country families of Kent and Sussex which provide a charming commentary on life in the smaller country houses in the years before the outbreak of the Civil War. In the work of Peter Oliver, who succeeded to his father Isaac's fashionable practice as a miniaturist, we find the same gentle sense of character and soft fullness of form. The style of Johnson and Peter Oliver could with safety be called increasingly English, and Mytens was painting at the English Court portraits that could hold their own with any comparable portraits being painted at that period on the Continent; but the potential development of English portraiture along the lines laid down by Mytens and Johnson was shattered by the impact of Van Dyck.

We shall always see through Van Dyck's eyes the King, his family and his courtiers. Our conception of the social life at the Caroline Court is deeply coloured by our knowledge of Van Dyck's commentary upon it. King Charles was not only, in Rubens' words, "the greatest amateur of paintings among the princes of the world": he had set himself to attract distinguished foreign artists to his Court. A number of lesser painters (such as Keirincx, Poelenburgh and Pot) worked for him for short periods; Gentileschi, Honthorst and Rubens came to London in the 1620's; and in Van Dyck the King found a portrait-painter admirably suited to his services: of wide experience, distinguished in person and manner and accustomed to moving in the most illustrious circles. He was a new phenomenon in English society.

As a painter Van Dyck provided for his successors a source of inspiration and a series of patterns and conventions which have still not been exhausted. From his earliest years as Rubens' most privileged student and assistant in Antwerp he had been a painter of rare brilliance, with a refinement and nervous delicacy that enabled him later so admirably and so subtly to record the transient security and fragile elegance of King Charles's Court. At his studio in Blackfriars he had to cope with an increasing fashionable practice. Many of Van Dyck's portraits show the lassitude of an over-wrought painter, and he was compelled to organize a team of assistants to turn out a large number of canvases by methods of production that were to be developed and perfected by Lely and Kneller.

Van Dyck's portraits with their changing moods must have given the King and his more sensitive courtiers the intensest pleasure. Where the subject required it, Van Dyck's touch could be nervous and incisive and his sense of tone (especially in his silvers and pinks) appropriately light and delicate; on other occasions his paint is rich, juicy and direct. He could create a state portrait, rich in echoes of Titian, with all the formal accessories of baroque portraiture perfectly controlled and inter-related; in his portraits of women (Pl. 17) and children he evoked, in a subtly aristocratic mannered style, a fragile charm which only Gainsborough was fully to understand. There is in almost all Van Dyck's English portraits an air of infinite remoteness, but he was sometimes inspired to paint, of such patrons whom he knew well as the King or Lord Strafford, a penetrating and sympathetic analysis of character. His spectacular double portraits and groups have a magnificent air of parade and his interest in landscape (which is shown in a handful of exquisite drawings) enabled him on occasion to set his sitters wholly within an open-air context (a form of portraiture which was to be developed in the eighteenth century) instead of placing them against the conventional backcloths of Van Somer or Mytens. Northumberland as Lord High Admiral stands contemptuously on the sea-shore; Lord Denbigh in Oriental costume lurches into a glade with his fowling-piece and starts back as he sees a brightly-coloured parrot. It is this new understanding of the relation of the sitter to a chosen context, and a new ease, informality and variety of pose, that set Van Dyck off so entirely from his predecessors and potential rivals in England and make him the immediate precursor of Reynolds and Gainsborough.

The impact of Van Dyck's style on painters working in England was instant and profound and the years immediately after his death in 1641, on the eve of the Civil War, produced a very large number of portraits cast in his patterns and painted in an almost invariably crude imitation of his handling. Even during his lifetime painters who had worked in the Anglo-Netherlandish manner were overwhelmingly influenced by the brilliant sophistication of Van Dyck's mature style. Johnson's later full-lengths, in particular, show an unashamed and oddly incongruous attempt to take over Van Dyck's conventional accessories and mannerisms; and Adriaen Hanneman, a gifted young Dutch painter who had worked in London since 1626, was back in The Hague in 1637 and imported into Holland an exaggeratedly Van Dyckian style. Amongst English painters Robert Walker, who was paradoxically the favourite painter of the Parliamentarian party during the Civil War and Interregnum, showed the most slavish dependence on Van Dyck; a certain angular sincerity only partly conceals the paradox of portraits of the regicides in patterns borrowed directly from Van Dyck's images of the King and his supporters.

To see William Dobson as the antithesis to Walker is to do him an injustice. His working life as we know it was pathetically short (nothing is known of his work before 1642 and he died in 1646), and he worked in the unsettling atmosphere of the war-time Court at Oxford. Nevertheless he was the most arresting and individual native portrait-painter "in large" in the Stuart period and probably the most distinguished English painter before the advent of Hogarth. His debt to Van Dyck was limited and controlled, and he had clearly studied the *tenebristi* painters of Italy and the North and the Venetian pictures in the great Caroline collections. He was a gentleman by birth and he was interested in problems which appealed to no other English painter in the century. His most elaborate compositions sometimes seem to be over-ambitious and his learning (in, for example, the use in his backgrounds of reliefs which would point to his sitter's tastes or occupation) is sometimes a little ponderous; but he painted for the royalist officers the only truly English baroque portraits: direct and uncompromisingly English in mood, filled with allegory and allusion, painted in a full-blooded, virile technique; rich in colour; and charged with a sense of the tragedy which they so vividly evoke (Pl. 14A).

His portraits, and their indication of the influences that he had been able to absorb, give us a glimpse of the effects which the enthusiasms of the "Whitehall group" of patrons and collectors might have had on painting (and indeed on architecture and sculpture) in this country if the Civil War had not shattered the brittle fabric of the Caroline Court where those enthusiasms had been stimulated. In landscape painting neither the Dutch painters, such as Keirincx, Poelenburgh and Stalbempt, who had worked in England in a form of Italo-Netherlandish, late Mannerist, style, nor Rubens and Van Dyck, who were amongst the most modern landscape painters in Europe, had formed a school of landscape painting in England; and throughout the Stuart period a predominating passion for topography, though it produced much very interesting material, prevented painters from exploring the English scene more deeply. In the field of decorative painting, however, Charles I's employment of Gentileschi, Vouet and Rubens, and his collection of Italian *cinquecento* pictures, bore fruit in the decorative schemes initiated, for example, by his courtiers William Murray, at Ham House in the 1630's, and the fourth Earl of Pembroke at Wilton in the closing years of the Civil War. In the Green Closet or Miniature Room at Ham, and even more in the Double Cube Room at Wilton, painting is made to play its part, with architecture and sculpture (or carving), in the evolution of a sumptuous baroque interior. The painting is far more ambitious and modern (with its clumsy echoes of Raphael, Polidoro and Rubens) than the monotonous repetition of standard decorative motives with which English homes and palaces had formerly been embellished.

There were a number of much less distinguished painters at work in London and the provinces, painting portraits which lack the sophistication of the work of their more successful and cosmopolitan contemporaries. Such painters are Thomas Leigh, John Souch, Gilbert Jackson and Edward Bower. Their portraits have a *gaucherie*, a naïve decorative quality or an archaizing flavour, even when they show the influence of Johnson, Mytens or Van Dyck, which enhance the ingenuousness and lack of affectation or technical skill with which the sitter's personality is set before us. And their portraits clearly represent the forms of painting which were available to all but the richest or most cultivated patrons. It was only at the Court, moreover, that a painter such as Van Dyck was commissioned or encouraged to paint subject pictures, and the Civil War inevitably hardened the "transalpine barbarous neglect" with which English patrons were inclined to regard any other form of painting than the portrait.

Peter Lely apparently met with little success in painting, on his arrival in this country from his native Holland (probably about 1645), "*Landtschapes*, with small *Figures* and *Historical Compositions*" in a nostalgic Dutch manner with strong reminiscences of Poelenburgh and Both. Thereafter he wisely concentrated on portraiture. By 1647 he was working for some of Van Dyck's former patrons; he was already described in 1654 as "the best artist in England"; and by the time of the Restoration, when he officially inherited Van Dyck's position at Court, his reputation was made. Until his death in 1680 he remained the leading fashionable portrait painter in England.

In Lely's portraits the influence of Van Dyck was very strong, but although his vigorous handling and fine sense of colour set him, after the death of Dobson, above any other painter working in England, he did not fully assimilate his great predecessor's example until the eve of the Restoration. At that time he produced his finest portraits (Pl. 14B) : with a Van Dyckian ease at last fused with his innate

Dutch feeling for volume, and of an entirely personal richness and purity of tone. They are the most distinguished reinterpretations of Van Dyck to be painted in this country in the seventeenth century.

Lely's practice was considerably larger than Van Dyck's and from the early 1660's he relied increasingly on the highly organized team of assistants who worked with him in his studio in Covent Garden and who could repeat over and over again, for different sitters, the patterns, with their increasing artificialities, which Lely evolved. The extreme familiarity of Lely's female beauties, who, with perennial fascination, seem to recapture the jaded splendours of the Court of Charles II and were eagerly sought after for their houses and galleries by collectors in Lely's lifetime, has eclipsed the greater qualities in Lely's achievement: his ability, in the freshness and timidity of his earlier portraits (Pl. 13B) and in some of the more deeply felt portraits of his maturity, to present a sympathetic or attractive analysis of his sitter's personality, and his great powers as a technician. In his compositions he was almost invariably content to rely on the heritage of Van Dyck, but in his later years his handling became more impressionist, and his last portraits are painted in a technique which was the fruit of many years' experience and which no pupil or imitator could wholly understand.

The Dutchman, Willem Wissing, was the pupil best qualified to inherit Lely's fashionable clientèle and to serve them with repetitions of the mannerisms and affectations that Lely evolved in his later Court style, which were common to all fashionable painters in London in the 1680's. Lely's most formidable rivals were probably those with the least ability, the French or Italian painters who were so popular in the open or latent Catholic atmosphere of the Courts of Charles II and James II: the Vignon brothers, Simon Verelst or Henri Gascars, whose work represents the nadir of contemporary French Court portraiture but was very popular with the Francophile element at Court; or Benedetto Gennari, the nephew of Guercino, who was a *protégé* of Mary of Modena and produced for a most distinguished circle of patrons at Court religious and mythological canvases and tastelessly elaborate portraits of unpleasant texture. Jacob Huysmans may also, for a short time, have been a more formidable rival. His more ambitious canvases are almost as unpleasant and vapid as Gennari's, but he was capable of greater sincerity with less intimidating or exigent clients.

Two painters stand outside Lely's orbit: his fellow-countryman Gerard Soest and the Scotsman Michael Wright. Wright, a less distinguished craftsman, remained essentially an amateur with interests outside his work as a painter, but a number of years spent in Rome and elsewhere on the Continent often gave to his canvases an educated cosmopolitan air. Soest's unusual sense of colour, his mannerisms in drawing, and his grave, introspective heads are sometimes reminiscent of Terborch, and, although he was never at ease with conventional society patrons, he could, when faced with a more interesting and sympathetic sitter (Pl. 15B),

c

produce a portrait of a haunting individuality beyond the powers of the more cynical Lely. Wright's sense of character remained, despite his travels, unmistakably British and he never entirely overcame a provincial inability to assemble more than the simplest form of composition. There is a charmingly unspoilt freshness in his presentation of character. Neither Soest nor Wright had Lely's technical abilities, but their handling is unmistakable: Soest's thin and shadowed and creating strange inflated masses of draperies; Wright's cooler and drier, but light and liquid in the treatment of details. Wright was almost certainly a Catholic and was much patronized by Catholic families: Bagots, Howards, Arundells of Wardour and Stonors are to be found amongst his sitters. There can be no doubt that the difficulties of his later years were made no easier by the increasing success of the arrogant young German, Godfrey Kneller.

Kneller had been extremely fortunate in the premature deaths of Wissing in 1686 and John Riley in 1691. The unhappy Riley, indeed, seems to have made little mark before Lely's death in 1680 and later to have been outshone by Kneller. He was not so capable a painter as his foreign rivals, and was often content to make use of their patterns; he was only rarely (and then in a very arresting manner) wholly at ease in compositions grander than a head and shoulders, and on a larger canvas he relied, at one period, on the facile collaboration of Closterman; but his individual cool silvery colour, light touch and gentle, ingenuous sense of character are at times reminiscent of Cornelius Johnson and the temper of his portraits is wholly English (Pl. 15A). He handed on these qualities of tone, character and touch, and an engaging provincialism, to his followers, Thomas Murray, Jonathan Richardson (Pl. 16A) and (to a lesser extent) Sir John Medina. Murray and Richardson remained almost unaffected by Kneller and, like their master, are seen at their best, with very rare exceptions, in portraits on a small scale; Murray was a much weaker painter than Riley and Richardson's portraits are often clumsy and coarse. But Richardson, as something of a scholar, and as a professional critic and theorist, did much to enhance the dignity of his profession (of which he was inordinately conscious) and has the distinction of being at the source of one of the streams that were to be an inspiration to the young Joshua Reynolds.

Godfrey Kneller was admirably qualified for the great position he held as the leading portrait painter in England, and one of the most successful in Europe, from the Revolution until his death in 1723. As a very young man in Holland he had come into contact with Bol, and possibly with Rembrandt himself, and he is said to have had some success in Italy, where he may have met Maratti and Bernini. By 1677, soon after his arrival in this country, he had gained introductions into the most illustrious circles and his success may well have been a formidable challenge to Lely in his last years. There is in Kneller's earliest English work a confusion between French, Dutch, Roman and Venetian influences and he also made use of Lely's patterns. These portraits are dry and thin and tend towards a brownish monochrome. By the early and mid-1680's, however, his canvases show a new directness in modelling, and in his best portraits of this period there is a lean, austere informality (Pl. 34B) which must have been very refreshing to patrons who had for so long been accustomed to Lely's lush, full-blown style.

Kneller painted Charles II and produced the official portraits of English sovereigns from James II to George I and his heir; many distinguished foreign visitors and European sovereigns, amongst them Louis XIV and Peter the Great, had sat to him in London, Paris and Flanders; and a monument in Westminster Abbey, embellished with an epitaph by Pope, crowned a career rich in worldly success. The organization of a small army of specialized assistants was perfected by Kneller in his studio in Great Queen Street. The steady output under his authority of a mass of competent but perfunctory work has done almost irreparable harm to his later reputation. But his best portraits are varied, penetrating, original and, in many cases, brilliantly painted. Although he was never so fine a colourist as Lely, in his best pieces his touch was fresh and incisive and his sense of tone pure and silvery. He was not afraid of painting portraits on a scale far more ambitious than Lely had attempted, and his full-lengths and equestrian portraits show a range unknown in England since the death of Van Dyck. And in a comparatively small number of portraits, some of them from his earlier years, Kneller broke away from the conventions which Van Dyck had established or popularized and to which Lely had remained almost consistently faithful, and, with an economical technique and unexpected powers of getting at the mind of his sitters, produced portraits of a new vigour or sympathy which would do credit to Hogarth or of a noble reserve which anticipates Reynolds.

In the reign of James II and the earliest years of William III Kneller's portraits still had something of the rich colour and the elaborate stagecraft that ultimately derive, through Lely's latest style, from Van Dyck's most formal English portraits; in the 1690's his more ambitious pieces sometimes have a sombre grandeur that may contain a reminiscence of his Roman years; but in the early years of the eighteenth century there is a new and rococo atmosphere in his portraits: light and silvery in key, gay and light-heartedly affected in design, soft and loose in handling. The same mood is felt in the portraits of his most talented rival, the Swede Michael Dahl. Kneller's portraits of the Kit-Cat Club proclaim that he was, at least intermittently, a Whig: Dahl was a favourite painter in Tory families. His more stereotyped female portraits are often unblushing repetitions, in a few standard patterns, of the most tiresome affectations of an age which saw the nadir of the Van Dyck tradition, but his feeling for character ranges from the weather-beaten old heads of his admirals, which hang beside the works of Kneller at Greenwich, to rather wistful portraits of children and young women. His later portraits are painted in soft, pastel-like tones of pink, silver, light blue and grey, and their fluttering movement and lightness of touch come near to the more completely rococo painters, such as Mercier and Van Loo, in the reign of George II.

It would be impossible in so short a survey to analyse in any detail the host of minor portrait painters who could turn their hands to a variety of tasks, some of a very humble nature, in London and the provinces during the second half of our period. There is, indeed, less temptation to do so than in its earlier years: some native painters such as Thomas Sadler or John Wollaston worked in a naïve manner which shows practically no advance from the days of Jackson and Bower. The fashionable conventions of portrait painting in the big London studios can be tiresome enough with painters as skilled as Lely or Kneller, and are irredeemably depressing in the hands of their imitators. It is only important to realize the debt to Lely of painters who flourished in the provinces, such as Matthew Dixon or Mr Comer, or of the hardworking but uninspired amateur, Mary Beale, in London, and to recognize the influence of Kneller on such lesser contemporaries as Jacques D'Agar or Thomas Gibson. None of the painters who remained rather outside the influence of Lely and Kneller (such as the two Kersebooms or the later members of the Verelst family) produced work of quality.

Dixon and D'Agar seem to have had a circle of clients in Northamptonshire and Comer was working in York for a number of years. Wissing was a favourite painter in country houses in the neighbourhood of Stamford and died at Burghley whilst he was at work on a large family group of the Cecils in hunting costume in which he "Seven-Times one great Perfection drew";[1] Michael Wright found time to spend some months in the 1670's working for the Bagots in Staffordshire and even Lely "spent some time at Gentlemen's houses" in the neighbourhood of Bury St Edmunds. In these country houses and in the capital, drawing and painting were becoming, in the hands of such enthusiasts as Mrs Pepys, the minor poetess Anne Killigrew, Lady Bathurst or the Princess of Orange, one of the favourite accomplishments of ladies of leisure that it has remained ever since. The only amateur painter of distinction in the Stuart period was the country gentleman, Sir Nathaniel Bacon, whose few surviving and arresting portraits are closely related to the Anglo-Netherlandish style of Johnson or Mytens.

The appearance and temperament of English men and women is perhaps best suggested in miniatures by Samuel Cooper and engravings and drawings by Loggan; their work, in its excellence and limitations, was essentially English. A more cosmopolitan glamour was occasionally given to a family's growing collection of portraits when its members brought back from their travels portraits of themselves that had been painted abroad. There is a fascination in seeing on the walls of an English house portraits of English travellers and diplomats painted in Holland by Miereveld, Lievens, Maes or Netscher; in France, especially if they were attached to the exiled Stuart Court at St Germains, by such French painters

[1] Matthew Prior, *Dialogues of the Dead* . . ., ed. A. R. Waller (1907), p. 32.

as Belle, Rigaud or Largillierre; and in Italy by Massimo Stanzione, Salvator Rosa, Carlo Dolci or Carlo Maratti. The less transitory experiences in Rome early in the eighteenth century of such young English artists and noblemen as William Kent, Lord Burlington and Thomas Coke were to be of profound significance for the structure of patronage and the history of the arts at home; but already, before the stricter standardization of tastes and enthusiasms in the Hanoverian age, classical influences had affected the outlook of the more sensitive Englishmen on the Grand Tour and found expression in pictures painted for them in England. Closterman could paint equally easily in a Flemish or Spanish idiom, but he was sent to Rome by Shaftesbury in 1699 and on his return produced portraits of his patron, in the full Roman manner, that could well serve as illustrations to the *Characteristicks*.

This cosmopolitanism was by no means a universal element in English taste and may often have been imitative and fashionable rather than thoughtfully formulated. Later to be so savagely attacked by Hogarth, it was already resented and opposed by such reactionary bodies as the Painter-Stainers' Company. Their efforts to vindicate native talent were triumphantly successful only at the very end of our period, when, early in the reign of George I, Sir James Thornhill wrested from his more facile and gifted foreign rivals the two leading commissions for decorative painting. Previously, in the reign of Charles II, such English decorative painters as Isaac Fuller and Robert Streeter had played second fiddle to their foreign rivals and had spent much of their time painting scenery for the stage.

The scope and quantity of decorative painting in this country between the reigns of Charles II and George I, and Thornhill's achievements in this context, are most significant for the English attitude to the full baroque style of the Continent and for the effect of the Grand Tour on the tastes which English patrons wished to gratify in their own homes. Extensive painting on walls and ceilings was of course primarily required in public buildings, such as the Hospitals at Greenwich and Chelsea, or in the royal palaces. Private patrons would often be content with a limited area of painted decoration, on ceiling, wall or staircase, enclosed in a raised carved or moulded framework: Laguerre and a team of interior decorators worked in this way for George Vernon on the ceilings of the parlour, saloon and staircase at Sudbury Hall between 1691 and 1694, and there are earlier examples of the same practice in the Duchess's Bedroom and Queen's Closet at Ham House. The full baroque panoply of painted ceilings and walls, often throughout a suite of rooms, on a staircase or in a private chapel, was almost invariably (though Thornhill's work at Stoke Edith was a remarkable exception) commissioned by patrons from a very limited class: by such noblemen of taste and discrimination as the fifth Earl of Exeter, who wished to recreate at Burghley House some of the splendours which he had admired on his travels, or by such great subjects as the first Duke of Devonshire and the Duke of Marlborough, who found in the full baroque style of Rome or Versailles the perfect means of decorating their magnificent new houses with an expression and a glorification in paint of the great achievements of their country or of their own parts therein.

In England the first complete example on a considerable scale of the baroque interior, relying on the close co-operation of architect, sculptor and decorative painter, was initiated at Windsor Castle by Charles II, partly in emulation of his cousin's activities at Versailles. The painted decoration, which contributed greatly to the lavish brightness of the new interiors, was entrusted in the main to the Leccese painter, Antonio Verrio, who first brought to this country a new repertory of decorative conventions and motives. His work at Burghley is perhaps his finest achievement: gay and festive and a most attractive embellishment of a fine set of late seventeenth-century interiors. His work retains an Italian lightness of mood and tone, but the devices by which Verrio extended in the imagination the actual space defined by the walls and ceilings of the rooms are predominantly French in inspiration. Verrio, and to a greater extent Laguerre, were deeply influenced by the methods evolved by Le Brun for the decoration of the Louvre, Vaux-le-Vicomte and, above all, Versailles: methods that in turn owed much to such Italian baroque painters as Pietro da Cortona and Romanelli. Verrio's two principal means of piercing a ceiling and its coving, to open a vista to the sky above, can be traced back to Le Brun. But an Italian prototype should perhaps be sought for his most ambitious device, in such rooms as the "Heaven" Room at Burghley House, where the entire surface of the room is painted with an elaborate feigned architectural structure, through, above and around which Verrio's gods and goddesses pour and tumble. The actual construction of Verrio's feigned prosceniums and painted architecture is always convincing; his imitation gilt, bronze and stucco are thoroughly effective; and his assistants were competent painters of still-life and flowers. It is only in the actual figure compositions that Verrio's draughtsmanship proves to be lamentably inadequate for the lavish and ambitious inventions of which he was so prodigal.

Louis Laguerre, who probably came to England in 1684, had been apprenticed to Le Brun and much of his work, such as the ballroom at Burghley or the Grand Stairs at Petworth, has the dully academic competence of that school; but his finest work, which he executed for the Dukes of Devonshire and Marlborough, could hold its own with any of the painted decoration by Le Brun and his team at Versailles. In the Saloon at Blenheim (1719–20) Laguerre painted a grandiloquent, arid reinterpretation of Le Brun's designs for the walls and ceiling of Louis XIV's *Escalier des Ambassadeurs*. Between 1689 and 1694 he had been working for Devonshire at Chatsworth and his ceilings in four of his patron's five state rooms are closely integrated in the decoration of these nobly sumptuous interiors; with great ingenuity and carefully evolved illusionism Laguerre built up on the coving a feigned sculptural, architectural and painted support for the big painted framework on the ceiling itself, within which his mythological scenes are enacted (Pl. 16B). Laguerre's work at Chatsworth is more restrained, but richer, more ingenious and more convincing in its illusionism than any of Verrio's decorative schemes.

Thornhill was closely influenced by his two continental predecessors: one of the earliest rooms that he painted, probably in 1706–7, was the Sabine Room at Chatsworth. But there is perhaps a lightness of touch and a new delicacy of form, even though he worked within the conventions that Verrio and Laguerre had brought to England. The rococo elements in Thornhill's style are possibly due to the Venetian painters who came to London in the early years of the eighteenth century. On a very different scale Thornhill showed himself to be a charming draughtsman who left behind him more drawings than any other painter working in England under the Stuarts: drawings that reveal, like his sketches in oil, a teeming invention and a light and facile touch. These are qualities that were inevitably lost when his ideas were eventually transferred on to a wall or ceiling: at Blenheim, for example, Wimpole or Easton Neston.

In 1708 the Earl of Manchester returned from his embassy in Venice and brought back with him two of the principal decorative painters of the city whose music and painting had so greatly charmed him: Giovanni Antonio Pellegrini and Marco Ricci. They were joined later by Marco's uncle, Sebastiano Ricci. These Venetian painters were attracted to the country by the prospect of such important commissions as the painting of the dome of St Paul's Cathedral, and they must have presented a formidable challenge to Laguerre and such other decorative painters as Gerard Lanscroon or Louis Cheron, whose work at Powis, Drayton or Boughton was faithful to the older Anglo-French tradition. Marco Ricci was mainly employed in painting landscape overdoors, in a rich and picturesque style, at such houses as Castle Howard, but his uncle and Pellegrini covered the walls and ceilings of their patrons' houses in a style which discarded the older decorative conventions, with their elaborate architectural basis, in favour of a much more dramatic presentation or of a bright, unhampered sunlit fluency. Sebastiano Ricci's design for the first Duke of Portland's chapel at Bulstrode show, in the words of George Vertue, "a Noble free invention, great force of lights and shade, with variety & freedom, in the composition of the parts".[1] Pellegrini's most important work was for the Whig noblemen, Manchester and the third Earl of Carlisle, in the houses that were being remodelled or built for them by Sir John Vanbrugh at Kimbolton and Castle Howard. His painting in the chapel and boudoir, and especially on the staircase and little landing at Kimbolton, or in the hall and two of the burnt-out rooms at Castle Howard, has a wholly rococo quality and charm. Pellegrini and Sebastiano were in the forefront of the Venetian renaissance in which Tiepolo was to be the most prominent

[1] *Notebooks*, vol. iv, Walpole Soc., vol. xxiv (1936), pp. 47–8.

figure and which owed so much to a renewed appreciation of Veronese: there are
characters on Pellegrini's walls at Castle Howard and Kimbolton who could have
stepped down from the walls of the Villa Maser, and the presence of these painters
in England sets this country within the range of one of the most important and
seductive movements in eighteenth-century painting.

The influences that brought about this most spectacular phase in the history of
English decorative painting came entirely from the Catholic countries of Europe:
from Paris, Rome, Naples or Venice. The full baroque style, in which architecture,
painting and sculpture could proclaim the greatness of an absolute monarch such
as Louis XIV or the unbending doctrines of the post-Tridentine Catholic Church,
would obviously have excited the admiration and envy of Charles II and his
openly Catholic brother, and at Windsor and Whitehall the secular and religious
iconography which was produced for them by painters and sculptors would not
have been out of place in Rome, Versailles, Vienna or Madrid. Lord Exeter had
Jacobite leanings, but the other patrons of Verrio, Laguerre, Thornhill and the
Venetians were loyal Protestants and the most lavish of them were to be found
amongst the Whigs and the most convinced opponents of Louis XIV. The Dutch
influence in this period, however, though it was less spectacular, was more deep-
seated and productive and perhaps more congenial. And under the later Stuarts it
was primarily the visiting Dutch and Flemish painters who laid the foundations of
English achievements in the eighteenth century in the genres of landscape, marine
and sporting painting.

These genres were considered by such strict classicists as Lord Shaftesbury to be
less honourable than history painting and they were of course much less popular
than the portrait. In the Stuart period, moreover, they were often used to serve a
purely subsidiary purpose: landscapes of various kinds, sea-pieces, battle-pieces
and still-lifes were frequently painted to be set into the panelling of a room, over a
door or mantelpiece, thus fulfilling a decorative function in the design of an
interior. Examples of this practice can be seen at Drayton, Sudbury Hall and
Ham House. The second Earl of Peterborough set over the doors and fireplaces in
his newly decorated rooms at Drayton a most interesting series of canvases:
classical landscapes, probably by the Dutchman Hendrick Danckerts and including
a view of the Tiber and the Castel Sant' Angelo; mountainous landscapes with
picturesque torrents in the manner of Beerstraten; a very interesting set of topographical pieces that includes Greenwich and the Monument and, farther afield,
Pontefract, Edinburgh Castle, Holyroodhouse and the Bass Rock; two groups of
birds by Francis Barlow; and a remarkable set of equestrian medieval knights in
armour against classical backgrounds. The careful heraldry in these strange
pieces indicates that they were inspired, like the series of ancestral portraits
in the King's Dining Room at Drayton, by Peterborough's inordinate pride
of race.

Danckerts was perhaps the first professional landscape painter to work for a considerable period in England: turning his hand with equal facility and moderate competence both to straightforward topography and to classical landscapes which combine a Claude-like nostalgia with recollections of the buildings and prospects that Danckerts had studied in Italy and which were often intended to be set into panelling. Such purely decorative landscapes, or more exciting scenes in the tradition of Jacob Ruysdael or Salvator Rosa, were painted for English houses by Adriaen van Diest, Gerard van Edema and Marco Ricci. Their canvases, and the use to which they were put, anticipate the pieces painted in the eighteenth century for houses such as Saltram, Harewood, Osterley or Bedford House by Zucchi, Zuccharelli or Gainsborough.

Landscape painting in the Stuart period was still almost synonymous with topography: Danckerts's topographical views of England or Italy were very popular with patrons from Charles II and the Duke of York to Samuel Pepys, and Wenceslaus Hollar, whose vast output of drawings and etchings throws such light on the interests of educated Englishmen of that time, devoted much of his energies to topographical prints and drawings. The two most interesting topographical painters, however, were the Dutchman Leonard Knyff and the Fleming Jan Siberechts. The patient and industrious Knyff drew an extensive series of bird's-eye views of English royal and country houses; they were engraved by Johannes Kip for the *Nouveau Théâtre de la Grande Bretagne* (1707–8) and are an incomparable source for the architectural historian and the student of garden design. Knyff also painted on a much larger scale panoramas of English buildings in their surroundings: his particularly attractive view of Clandon (1708) provides a charmingly naïve anecdotal picture of the day-to-day life of a country house. Siberechts was a much more individual artist. His approach to the English scene and his treatment of country people, their dwellings and occupations remained fundamentally Flemish; his grander views of the English countryside and of houses such as Longleat or Wollaton have great charm, but are constructed in a standard topographical formula that was constantly exploited on the Continent, and especially in France by Van der Meulen or the Martins in their views of the French king's houses and campaigns. In subjects where he was perhaps less controlled by a patron's need for an accurate record of the house and garden, Siberechts created a freer and more sensitive impression of the English countryside: the spacious views from Richmond Hill or along the Trent, or a glade on a hillside with a glimpse of a great house below (Pl. 19). His water-colour drawings of the Peak District (1694, 1699) are, with Francis Place's later drawings, the most important premonitions of the English supremacy in this technique in the following century.

Kip, Knyff, Siberechts and lesser, mainly anonymous painters enabled the landed classes to secure drawn, painted or engraved records of their houses and estates. At Badminton a particularly interesting set of views survive of the first

Duke of Beaufort's house and of his other possessions and castles: a series that must have given special pleasure to so great a territorial magnate and to his Duchess, who later, in her widowhood, secured Knyff's services in showing "what a noble place my deare Lord has left". In a tentative manner these canvases at Badminton foreshadow the more sophisticated views of English castles and country houses by Canaletto, Richard Wilson or Marlow. The liveliest picture of social life in an English seventeenth-century village was provided by Gillis van Tilborch's fascinating *Tichborne Dole* (1670), where the villagers await the distribution of the hereditary charity at the hands of Sir Henry Tichborne, who stands surrounded by his family, retainers and servants in front of his Tudor house (Pl. 18B).

The origins of the sporting piece, a peculiarly English genre that was to achieve such rich expression in the eighteenth century, are to be found in the Stuart period. The only English painter to work for the Lauderdales at Ham (appropriately in the Volary) was Francis Barlow, the earliest professional English animal painter, who as early as 1652–3 was specializing in birds and fishes. He never acquired more than a limited sense of composition; his subjects and sense of narrative have an engaging provincialism; and he was technically a less distinguished painter of animals than Knyff or Abraham Hondius. But Barlow's creatures are most carefully and lovingly observed and his many drawings, some of them appropriately for an edition of Aesop's *Fables*, are the first sensitive studies by an Englishman of wild and domestic animals: his studies of hunting scenes, some of which were etched by Hollar for *Severall Wayes of Hunting, Hawking and Fishing* (1671), recapture something of the sylvan charm of the *Compleat Angler*. His drawings also provided Barlow with the material for his large canvases, such as those he painted for Denzil Onslow's house at Pyrford. These works, which hang today at Clandon, are a direct anticipation of the series of huge canvases of hunting scenes with which Wootton decorated the halls of Longleat, Althorp and Badminton in the time of George II.

John Wootton was a more accomplished painter and of much greater importance in the development of the English sporting piece. The greater part of his *œuvre* lies beyond our period, but he had already, by 1715, produced a number of life-size portraits of horses (at Clandon, Welbeck and Chatsworth) and one or two large, spacious and ambitious hunting scenes: Lady Henrietta Harley hawking and hunting and Lord Conway drawn up with his fellow-huntsmen on a vast canvas (1714) at Ragley. The most important precursors of these canvases are the huge portraits of horses that were painted, traditionally by Abraham van Diepenbeeck, for that great horseman the Duke of Newcastle and survive at Welbeck. Wootton's more mature sporting pieces are on a lesser scale and his smaller pictures, which are of such value as documents in a great age of horse-breeding, established conventions which survived to the days of Stubbs, Ben Marshall and beyond. Peter Tillemans, as a topographical and sporting painter, had a lighter and more rococo touch, but his compositions are less closely integrated than Wootton's.

It was not until comparatively late in his career, paradoxically, that Wootton seems to have come under the influence of Gaspar Poussin, Claude or Jan Wyck. Jan Wyck, who is recorded in London in 1674 and worked at Ham, painted battlepieces in the manner of Wouwermans and hunting scenes in a fluent style which directly foreshadows Wootton's (Pl. 18A). He also specialized in little equestrian portraits (a genre which had been neglected since the time of Van Dyck) which were of no less significance for his successors. His little portrait of Monmouth seems to have been accompanied by a set of canvases depicting moments in the Duke's career as a soldier in Scotland and the Low Countries (there are similar canvases by Wyck at Drayton). And, probably in 1672, there arrived in this country from Holland the two most distinguished naval painters of the age: Willem van de Velde, father and son. For nearly thirty years they worked in partnership to provide the royal brothers and naval commanders with records of their ships and the engagements in which they had taken part; these dramatic compositions and their spacious "calms" were of profound importance for such painters as Samuel Scott in the succeeding period. The Van de Veldes were indeed the fathers of marine painting in this country.

The importance to English painting of the Dutch influence in the lesser genres can hardly be over-estimated. Dutch pictures had been admired in England since at least the time of Charles I, who had owned works by Rembrandt, and in the later Stuart period certain types of Dutch painting were gaining a popularity which they have never lost: the microscopic realism and fine finish of the Dutch flower-piece and the exciting illusionism of perspective painting caused painters such as Simon Verelst and Samuel van Hoogstraaten to be much admired. Flower painting was already a favourite pastime for ladies and was developed professionally as a highly decorative genre, admirably suited for overdoors, by the prolific Frenchman Jean Baptiste Monnoyer, who worked almost exclusively for the first Duke of Montagu, and by the Hungarian Jakob Bogdani. Bogdani also specialized in animal and bird painting in the style of Hondecoeter: his fascinating record of the aviary formed in Windsor Park by Admiral George Churchill was bought by Queen Anne after the Admiral's death in 1710 and is now at Kew.

Although they were anathema to Lord Shaftesbury there is no doubt that "waggish Collectors, and the lower sort of *Virtuosi*" delighted in the subject-matter of pictures by Brouwer, Adriaen van Ostade or Jan Steen. The Dutch painter Egbert van Heemskerck worked with success in this vein at the end of the century: there is an instructive set of pieces by him at Birdsall which was probably painted for Sir Thomas Willoughby. His satirical pieces were to influence Hogarth's choice of subject-matter. In a different social context, hesitant efforts were being made by seventeenth-century painters such as Joan Carlile and

Stephen Browne at the conversation piece, a genre which Hogarth was to develop and which was to be so popular in the eighteenth century.

"In growing and enlarging times, Arts are commonly drowned in Action."[2] The Stuart period was this country's "growing and enlarging time" and the political, economic, social and religious upheavals of the age inevitably affected the development of the arts. For the fundamental issue is this: the ability of a country where religious and national prejudices were so strong to realize and to absorb influences from the Continent. The enthusiasm and cosmopolitan tastes of Charles I attracted to this country the greatest of all baroque painters and thus laid before English patrons new and infinitely sophisticated idioms which were to be a continuing source of inspiration. The arts of the Caroline Court evoked the hostility of reactionary and more simply Protestant minds, but by the end of the century, although there were iconoclastic outbreaks in 1688, increasing religious toleration and first-hand acquaintance with the arts of the Continent had done much to break down these older prejudices: Whig and Tory patrons could employ Catholic artists on Catholic subjects with no twinge to their consciences.

In English taste and in English painting the seventeenth century is a watershed. By 1700 engravings had brought a knowledge of the arts to circles far wider than those to which they were accessible in 1603. The lack of the regular and organized academic training, through which young Continental painters could pass, gave even to the finest native painting, the portraits of Cooper and Dobson, a freshness and independence and something of the amateur's unspoilt vision. Much English painting is exceedingly provincial and the native painter was often eclipsed by his more accomplished foreign rival: Greenhill or Riley could never achieve the facility of conception and execution of Lely, Wissing or Kneller, and only Thorn-hill had the experience to equal Verrio or Laguerre. But it was the foreign portrait painters, Mytens, Lely, Kneller, the foreign artists in the lesser genres, and above all Van Dyck, who brought to England continental experience and technical methods of a high order and who thus divide the archaisms of the Jacobean age from the achievements of Hogarth, Wilson, Reynolds, Gainsborough or Stubbs: achievements which were made possible by their predecessors under the Stuarts and by a growing realization that English painting could thrive only if patrons and artists alike were prepared to open their minds to the inspiration of European art.

[2] Sir Henry Wotton, preface to *Elements of Architecture* (1624).

SCULPTURE

MARGARET WHINNEY

ENGLISH sculpture in the Stuart period, though great in quantity, is much less distinguished in quality than either architecture or painting. Moreover, its scope is still limited mainly to tombs. The rich figure decoration of saints and angels in seventeenth-century continental churches was not approved in England and, until late in the century, there is relatively little external sculpture on secular buildings. Tomb sculpture had, however, a special appeal to Englishmen, for, like the painted portrait, it fostered the interest in the individual and the emphasis on the family. All classes of men, great landowners, scholars and merchants, ordered tombs either in their wills or before their death; they are to be found in countless country churches and they range from sumptuous architectural structures with many figures, through the simpler types with only an effigy of the owner, to wall tablets (often beautiful in design) which record a burial near by. From them a wonderfully clear picture can be obtained of changes in taste throughout the century.

At the beginning of the century tomb sculpture was largely in the hands of foreign craftsmen, Dutch and Flemish, most of whom had come to England as refugees during the sixteenth-century Wars of Religion. Their workshops (generally in Southwark on the south bank of the Thames) often lasted for two or three generations. Tombs made there were sent all over England. The work is usually competent, and the designs, broadly speaking, fall into two groups, one showing the effigy of the patron and his wife lying on their backs, with their hands joined in prayer, beneath a simple architectural canopy, the other having kneeling figures. The tomb of Sir Roger Aston at Cranford, Middlesex (d. 1612), by William Cure (Pl. 20), rich in coloured alabaster, is only one of a great number of the second type. Both patterns were to last down to the middle of the century, but gradually the handling and often the materials change. Nicholas Stone (1583–1647), about whom we know a great deal – his Note Book and Account Book have survived and show the daily working of his studio – was trained in one of the foreign workshops and later in Holland, but in 1619 he was made Master Mason at the Banqueting House at Whitehall, and so came into close contact with Inigo Jones. His tomb of Thomas, Lord Knyvett (Pl. 24A), at Stanwell, Middlesex, for which he was paid £215 in 1623, is quieter in colour and more refined in its handling of architectural detail than the Aston tomb, and the modelling of the figures is more sensitive and gracious. Stone had an enormous practice and made tombs of many different types. His best work has fine quality, but he employed many assistants and the "workshop pieces" are often a little dull. His association with the Court brought him into touch with the new Italian taste and also aroused his interest in the antique sculpture bought by Charles I. His monument to Francis Holles (d. 1622) in Westminster Abbey, the first to show an Englishman as a Roman hero, is modelled on Michelangelo's tomb of Guiliano de' Medici and several of his later works show figures with soft, clinging draperies imitating the antique.

Other mason-sculptors, such as Edward Marshall and Thomas Stanton, were less influenced by new ideas, though the former could produce work of good quality. Maximilian Colt of Arras, whose real name was Poultrain, is a puzzling figure. He was made Master Sculptor to James I, and executed for him the tomb of Queen Elizabeth I in Westminster Abbey. He also produced the unusual tomb of the first Earl of Salisbury (1614: Hatfield, Hertfordshire), its effigy on a bier supported by Virtues, and a skeleton beneath (Pl. 25A). Its type never became popular, though its use of contrasting black and white marble was to be widely copied. Colt's heavy figures lack refinement; his later tombs are dull; and he was only to obtain minor decorative commissions from Charles I.

Charles was, however, less lucky in the foreign sculptors he attracted than in his foreign painters. Hubert le Sueur, a Frenchman who first appears in England in 1625, had been in contact with distinguished Italian artists in France but, though he had learnt something of their methods, his own work is strangely dull. He is, however, of some importance in the history of English sculpture, for he brought new forms and new techniques. From about 1520 until the time of Le Sueur's arrival nearly all sculpture in England had been in alabaster or stone (though very occasionally marble was used). Le Sueur was a skilled worker in bronze; indeed he is far more accomplished as a craftsman than as a designer. His statue of the third Earl of Pembroke, now in the Schools Quadrangle at Oxford (Pl. 23), is pompous in pose and empty in the modelling of the head, but the detailed treatment of the armour is finely done. The same insensitive modelling appears in his best-known work, the statue of Charles I on horseback at Charing Cross. Le Sueur was also responsible for a development of the portrait bust. English mason-sculptors had used busts in a roundel, the shoulders cut by the frame, in church monuments, Nicholas Stone's *Sir Thomas Bodley* (1615: Merton College, Oxford) being a typical example. Le Sueur's bust monuments (for instance, the *Lady Cottington* in Westminster Abbey) are different in form, for the bust stands on a small pedestal, and so is related to the independent portrait busts common on the Continent in the sixteenth century, but very rare in England. Such portraits were also made by Le Sueur. The *Charles I* in antique armour, now at Stourhead (Pl. 22A), stood in the Chair room at Whitehall Palace; his bust of Archbishop Laud belongs to St John's College, Oxford. All his work has the same smooth modelling of the features, giving almost no feeling of the texture of the skin or of the precise form of the bony structure beneath it; the pose is always stiff and frontal, lacking vitality. Both the other foreign sculptors who worked for Charles I, Francesco Fanelli (who made the Diana Fountain in Bushey Park) and François Dieussart, were better artists, but neither was anywhere near the first rank, and the one major piece of sculpture connected with the King, his bust made by Bernini in Rome in 1636, perished in the fire at Whitehall in 1698.

The mason-sculptors of the first half of the century had many of them established workshops which passed to their sons or nephews, and much sound if rather uninspired work was done. After the Restoration, however, a new type of man appeared, who described himself as a "statuary" rather than a carver, and who had generally travelled. The first of these was John Bushnell (c. 1630–1701). Trained in an English workshop, he was forced because of domestic trouble to flee to the Continent. Several years were spent in Italy before his return in the late 1660's. During this time he saw, and clearly admired, Roman baroque sculpture with its drama and movement, its deeply undercut draperies, its brilliant exploitation of expression and of materials. His first works, the Stuart kings and a queen still on Temple Bar, or the statues of Charles I and Charles II from the Royal Exchange, now in the Old Bailey, make a valiant, though not completely successful, attempt to reproduce the Italian manner. His monument to Lord Mordaunt (d. 1675) in All Saints', Fulham (Pl. 24B), is perhaps his finest work. It is new in its use of a lively standing figure, and in its rejection both of an architectural frame and of all suggestion of Christian piety. Mordaunt is vigorous and alert, in white marble against the curved black background, his gauntlets and coronet on pedestals at the sides. The dramatic turning pose, the sweep of the cloak wrapped round the figure and deeply undercut, proclaim its baroque intention. A comparison of this figure with Le Sueur's Pembroke (Pl. 23) reveals at once the change of style. Bushnell's first works in or near London must have been a revelation to many English craftsmen; it is sad that he never fulfilled his early promise. As early as 1675, in the Ashburnham tomb at Ashburnham in Sussex, he shows an inability to convey the structure of the body; his work becomes progressively weaker, his mind deteriorated, commissions were left unfinished, and he died insane. He is also recorded as a maker of busts, and there is good reason to believe that the portrait of Charles II, of which the finished marble is at Melton Constable, Norfolk, and the preliminary terra-cotta (Pl. 22B) in the Fitzwilliam Museum, Cambridge, is his. The twist of the head, the rich and lively treatment of the curled wig and lace cravat, are again clear evidence of a knowledge of baroque art, and stress the contrast with the more conservative work done for Charles I (Pl. 22A).

Busts were evidently becoming more common, and not only among the great, for Pepys records how, on the 10th February, 1669, he had a lifemask taken, and the bust of his wife on her monument in St Olave's, Hart Street, is almost certainly by John Bushnell. Not many have survived, apart from monuments, the finest being the few made by Edward Pierce, who was one of the Master Masons of St Paul's Cathedral. His bust of Sir Christopher Wren (Ashmolean Museum, Oxford), dated 1673, is baroque in form, broad across the shoulders, with a loop of drapery falling over the chest, though the head is still frontal. The *Thomas*

Evans (Pl. 25B) of 1688, belonging to the Painter-Stainers' Company, London, is more vigorous in pose, with the head slightly turned and lifted. It is broadly and fully modelled and indeed, in its description of the features and its perception of the planes of the face, is superior to the Bushnell.

A rather different continental tradition is represented by the sculpture of Caius Gabriel Cibber (1630–1700) and Grinling Gibbons (1648–1721). Both use modified baroque types and draperies, but their figures (especially their female figures) are often heavily built with heads following the classical tradition. It seems probable that both were influenced by the work of the studio of Artus Quellin in Amsterdam, and it should perhaps be recalled that there is much Dutch influence to be found in England in other arts in the reign of Charles II. Cibber, a Dane by birth, had visited Italy, but almost his whole working life was spent in England, which he reached during the Commonwealth. He is first recorded as foreman in the workshop of John Stone, Nicholas Stone's son. He is known to have been in Holland with Stone, who had Dutch relations. His most ambitious work is the relief on the Monument, in London, an allegorical piece showing Charles II succouring the City after the Great Fire of 1666, but his most appealing is certainly the Sackville Monument (1677) at Withyham, Sussex (Pl. 21B). This is, in one way, a transformation of the old type of monument with kneeling figures but, instead of men and women kneeling in prayer, the parents are now shown on either side of a free-standing tomb, mourning their young son, who reclines between them. The spectator is inevitably drawn to join in their grief, and to this extent the conception is baroque; but there is none of the rhetoric of Bushnell's work, and the smoothly cut rounded figures are very Dutch in handling. Cibber was also responsible for garden figures at Belvoir and Chatsworth (a few garden figures, but not many, are known to have been made earlier in the century), and in the latter house he played his part in the ensemble of the chapel. The statues of Faith and Justice above the altar are his work, but compared with the adoring saints, or angels alighting from rapid flight, of Italian baroque art, they are markedly static in pose. He had, before he went to Chatsworth in 1688, made a fountain for Soho Square showing Charles II above the Four Rivers of England (parts of which survive), and the figures of Raving and Melancholy Madness, with their unforgettable realism, which adorned the gate of Bedlam Hospital, and are now in the Guildhall Museum. His last work was architectural decoration for Sir Christopher Wren; it included the pediment on the east front of Hampton Court Palace, showing the Triumph of Hercules, an allusion to William III's victories over Louis XIV. His career, therefore, gives clear enough evidence of the increased range of opportunity open to sculptors in the later years of the century, and, though his work is seldom very distinguished, it never falls below a fair standard of competence.

Grinling Gibbons is a more controversial figure. He was a brilliant wood-carver and it was here that his chief strength lay. But much sculpture of very varied quality was also produced by his studio. Some of it, for instance the bronze statue of James II now outside the National Gallery, is very fine; other figures, such as *The Duke of Somerset* in the Library of Trinity College, Cambridge, are almost grotesque in their clumsiness. Judging from an account written by George Vertue at the time of Gibbons' death, it was generally recognized by his contemporaries that he had no great ability in bronze or marble, and most of such work was carried out by assistants. Most important of these was Arnold Quellin, the son of the sculptor at Amsterdam, who worked with Gibbons from about 1681 until his early death in 1686. Most of the best large-scale figure sculpture which came from Gibbons' studio dates from these years, and it may be that such quality as it has

Two cherubs' heads carved in wood by
Grinling Gibbons in Trinity College,
Cambridge.

was due to Quellin, who in his monument to Thomas Thynne in Westminster Abbey proves that he had considerable ability as a designer. The tomb of Baptist Noel, Viscount Campden (Pl. 21A), erected in 1686 at Exton in Rutland, is the most lavish example of the work of these years. Like many tombs of the period, there is no direct Christian sentiment; Lord Campden and his wife, both in classical dress, stand on either side of an urn (always an emblem of mortality), whilst above is a tent-like drapery. The children, instead of kneeling below or beside their parent, as in the tombs of the first years of the century, are shown in conversation or at play in reliefs on the two flanking obelisks, and below the main figures. The latter have neither the vitality of Bushnell's Mordaunt, nor the sincerity of the parents in Cibber's Sackville tomb, but in their slightly theatrical poses are very typical of the work of Gibbons' studio at its best. His later tombs – Lady Newdigate at Harefield, Middlesex, or Sir Cloudesley Shovell in Westminster Abbey – are clumsy in their treatment of the figure; though sometimes in

D

Monument to Tobias Rustat (d. 1693),
in Jesus College Chapel, Cambridge,
probably by the workshop of Grinling
Gibbons.

a smaller scale work, such as the monument to Robert Cotton (1697: Conington, Cambridgeshire), with its portrait medallion within a wreath of flowers, he is more successful.

Another foreigner linked with this studio was Jan van Ost (or John Nost as he came to be called), who married Arnold Quellin's widow. Although he made a few tombs, he is chiefly known for his lead garden figures. Some, like those at Rousham, Oxfordshire, have a strange angular quality which is highly personal; others, at Melbourne, Derbyshire, or on the gateposts at Hampton Court, are charming chubby boys, based on good Italian models.

A purely English sculptor whose best work has considerable merit was Francis Bird (1667–1731), but he too was trained abroad, first in Brussels and then in Rome. The dates of many of his tombs are uncertain, but that of Dr Busby in Westminster Abbey (probably of about 1703) is greatly superior, both in design and cutting, to any marble monument by Gibbons. It would seem that Sir Christopher Wren also had a good opinion of Bird, since he chose him to make his daughter's monument, and also to carve the dramatic scene of the Conversion of St Paul on the west front of the Cathedral. This is difficult to see, much weathered, and is therefore usually under-rated. Bird's designs are often novel. His ambitious late works are outside our period; but his bust monument to Sir Orlando Gee (c. 1705: Isleworth, Middlesex) has a lively baroque portrait which includes the hands, a pattern new to England.

Several other English sculptors of ability – Richard Crutcher, Thomas Green of Camberwell and Thomas Stayner – were producing work of good quality in the early years of the eighteenth century, and there were also competent men in the provinces. In the case of many elaborate, ambitious tombs the artists are still un-identified. And, in addition, there is a great quantity of attractive work on a more modest scale. The innumerable wall tablets, without figures, though often with beautifully designed shields, drapery, cherubs' heads, skulls or flowers, bear witness both to the good level of English craftsmanship and also to the wish for com-memoration felt by men of all classes.

EARLY GEORGIAN

PAINTING

HUGH HONOUR

"We are now arrived at the period in which the arts were sunk to the lowest ebb in Britain", wrote Horace Walpole of the reign of George I. It was with greater complacency that he entered upon "a more shining period in the history of arts" which opened with the accession of George II, for, though painting "made but feeble efforts towards advancement. . . The reign was not closed when Sir Joshua Reynolds ransomed portrait painting from insipidity". Walpole was writing with the critic's usual contempt for the taste of the previous generation, but his assessment of the age may still be acccepted. In 1714 Kneller was at the height of his popularity, and within a year he was awarded the baronetcy which proved to be the highest honour conferred upon a painter until Leighton was ennobled. Before the period had closed Reynolds, Wilson and, less conspicuously, Gainsborough had given clear indications of their ability. Essentially an age of transition, it spans the career of only one painter of outstanding importance, William Hogarth, whose complex personality reflects all the conflicting currents of the time.

Sir Godfrey Kneller's importance in 1714 can scarcely be exaggerated and his declining influence lasted throughout the period. Even so late as 1752 John Ellis, the King's painter, is said to have exclaimed, on seeing a portrait by the young Reynolds, "This will never answer. You don't paint in the least degree in the manner of Kneller. ... Shakespeare in poetry and Kneller in painting, dammee." The first artist to make a fortune out of painting portraits in Britain, Kneller was as ostentatiously successful as lordly manners, fine carriages and an army of attendants could show, and those who wished to emulate his social achievement followed his artistic practices. Perhaps his worst effect on English painting was in his establishment of a staff of assistants, not students, highly qualified to execute the different parts of a portrait – the peruque, the lace cravat, the coat, the background curtain – whilst the master confined his attention to the face. Only three of the notable portrait painters of this period – Hogarth, Highmore and strangely enough John Ellis – eschewed this business-like practice. Joseph Van Aken, the most widely employed drapery painter, consequently assumed an important rôle in the history of portraiture, leading Horace Walpole to remark that "as in

England almost everybody's picture is painted, so almost every painter's works were executed by Van Aken". Occasionally the process was, so to speak, reversed; John Wootton employed a face-painter to complete equestrian portraits and George Lambert relied upon associates for the figures in his landscapes.

It would, however, be mistaken to assume that Kneller's influence was wholly unfortunate. His worldly success did much to raise the social standing of the artist who could, when sufficiently prosperous, move on terms of familiarity with the professional classes. The Academy he founded was responsible for training many painters of note, including Hogarth, and was the ancestor of the Royal Academy schools. But his most important legacy was in his rich, sensuous handling of paint; it distinguished his followers from men such as Richardson, Ramsay and Hudson who preferred a smooth texture.

Foreign influences. Foreign influences on English painting persisted throughout the eighteenth century, but their nature changed towards the end of our period. The early eighteenth-century painter went abroad to study under a master from whom he might learn some "tricks of the trade", to copy Old Masters for his patron's gallery and to acquire that diploma of fashion which foreign travel alone could give. William Kent studied under Benedetto Luti and Francesco Solimena, Allan Ramsay under Solimena and Imperiali. But when Reynolds went to Italy in 1750 he turned a blind or unappreciative eye on his contemporaries and gave his undivided attention to the earlier painters, to Raphael, whom he parodied in a caricature, to Michelangelo, to Albani and Guido Reni. In so doing he was merely following the aristocratic taste of the time, which had grown steadily more antiquarian as the century proceeded, and he would have been in full agreement with those travellers who based their standards on Jonathan Richardson's useful guide to the *Statues, Bas-reliefs, Drawings and Pictures in Italy*. It was indeed the writings of Richardson that had fired him with the ambition to be more than an "ordinary painter".

Contemporary foreign influence came principally from France, and its elegant refinement, popularized by the engraver, Gravelot, flourished in the work of Philip Mercier, himself a German of French extraction, Hayman, the young Gainsborough and, to a limited extent, Hogarth. Moreover, foreign artists set up their studios in England – the history painter Jacopo Amigoni, the portrait painters J. B. Van Loo and Andrea Soldi, the bird painters Pieter Casteels and Honde-cooter, the *vedutiste* Canaletto and Antonio Joli – providing native artists with for-midable rivals for the favours of the fashion-conscious patron. Influences from the past were more varied and derived principally from Holland and Italy. Claude Lorraine, Salvator Rosa and Gaspar Poussin exerted an almost crushing influence on decorative landscapes. The Dutch tradition of marine painting as practised by the Van de Veldes was followed by Peter Monamy and Samuel Scott. Dutch, as well as Italian landscapes, informed Richard Wilson, who confessed a debt to Cuyp, whilst Gainsborough learned from and copied Ruysdael and Wynants. Nor were Dutch genre pictures without their influence on Hogarth, whose attitude to the old "dark" masters was ambivalent. Whilst he travestied several of their famous figures in his prints, satirized their cult (Pl. 27B) and painted *Sigismunda* to prove that a modern Briton could equal a seventeenth-century Italian, he was not above plundering their works more slyly to add dignity to a history picture or even a portrait.

The British school. Out of this mixture, this "ragout" of foreign styles and influences, there slowly emerged the British school of painting, whose growth was largely determined by two factors, a spirit of nationalism and a desire for greater truth to nature. In the literary and artistic history of the early Georgian period no movement is more important than that of nationalism, or rather growing national self-consciousness, which found its most notable expression in the novels of Fielding, the paintings of Hogarth, the architecture of the Burlingtonians and, finally, the gothic revival. It accounts to a great extent for the change which came over landscape painting when it was realized, in Horace Walpole's words, that "because Virgil gasped for breath at Naples, and Salvator wandered among Alps and Apennines", there was no reason why "our ever-verdant lawns, rich vales, fields of haycocks and hop grounds" should be neglected by poet or painter. Its least attractive form is found in the arrogant, Squire Westernish attitude displayed by Hogarth when he advised the student to beware of Italy because it would seduce him from nature. But Hogarth was not alone in this opinion, and the more moderate George Stubbs declared that he went to Italy in 1754 only "to convince himself that nature was and always is superior to art, whether Greek or Roman – and having received this conviction, he immediately resolved upon returning". The nationalist movement was best expressed by those artists who eschewed the airs and graces of the continental schools for the ideal of "nature". In part they continued the native tradition of John Riley, in part they reacted from the baroque style of Kneller. Portrait painters such as Hogarth, Highmore and, at times, Richardson approached their subjects with less formality and greater directness; such landscape painters as George Lambert began to abandon the decorative variations of Gaspar Poussin for scenes derived from the English countryside.

In direct opposition to the antiquarian taste of the aristocracy, the naturalist movement owed much of its success to the increasing patronage of a middle class enriched by the years of Whig supremacy. Many of the best portraits executed during the period were of middle-class sitters, and the conversation piece was established mainly because of its popularity with those who could neither afford nor house larger works. Above all, William Hogarth displayed both the merits and the prejudices of the middle class, on whose patronage he principally relied for his portraits and prints of modern moral subjects. The growing popularity of prints is itself a symptom of a widening appreciation of the arts. John Smith and the young John Faber appear to have found a not inconsiderable market for mezzo-tints after fancy pieces and portraits of celebrities. Like Hogarth's moral subjects, Highmore's illustrations to *Pamela* – the epitome of middle-class values – and most of Mercier's late works were painted primarily for reproduction in en-gravings. Such prints found their way into all manner of houses, from the great Palladian mansions to the small town house and country box.

In the greatest houses old masters, whether original or copies, were the rule which was broken only in favour of such works as the ancients could not supply: that is to say, portraits, topographical views of the owner's domains and decorative paintings which might take the form of vast ceilings or small landscapes let into the walls above doors and chimney-pieces. The relative importance given to such works is exemplified by the catalogue Horace Walpole made of his father's pictures at Houghton in 1743. Expatiating at length on the unequalled collection of works by Carlo Maratti, Guido Reni, Claude, Domenichino and others, he mentions portraits mainly with reference to their subjects and remains all but silent about William Kent's ceilings.[1] The great house would usually contain a fairly large number of portraits, some decorative views and a few topographical landscapes by English painters. In smaller homes the pictures would be limited almost exclusively to portraits which were mainly the work of itinerant journey-men.

William Hogarth. Before proceeding to the various types of painting executed in this period we must consider the work of William Hogarth, who essayed all of them except landscape. No single artist reflects the various aspects of the period more clearly, and yet none, in his total achievement, was more revolutionary. When his borrowings from, and parodies of, Italian masters have been pains-takingly detected, when his xenophobic attitude has been examined, when his moralism has been analysed and his aesthetic theory discounted, the artist remains, perplexing, alluring, always one of the most popular and sometimes one of the best of English painters. Truculently emerging from his apprenticeship as an en-graver in 1728, he quickly made a name for himself, but never secured the highest patronage; unquestionably the best English and one of the best European artists of his time, he founded no school and his subsequent influence has been spasmodic.

The keenness and directness of Hogarth's vision are evident in all his work, in portraits no less than genre scenes. Although by no means the first artist to abandon the social mask for portraiture, no one had before combined a truth to nature so ruthless with psychological penetration so deep. His one grand portrait, the full length of Captain Coram (Pl. 31) which he presented to the Foundling

---

[1] It should, however, be remembered that Horace Walpole had a just contempt for Kent's paintings.

Hospital in 1740, was based on a baroque portrait by Rigaud, but has nothing grandiose about it; the kindly, beaming philanthropist has been painted in such a way that he is neither undignified nor standing on his dignity. It is one of the great landmarks in the history of English painting, for, as Professor Waterhouse has remarked, Captain Coram "is no longer a type with individual features, but an individual in his own right, whose character is reflected in those features". All his portraits are of individuals, not least the group of his servants (National Gallery) which he painted with such rare tenderness and understanding. But his frankness and keen perception of character did not recommend him to the wealthier patrons, who demanded a modicum of flattery. Even in the group portrait of David Garrick and his wife (the Royal Collection) he has made no effort to disguise, or emphasize, the slightly vulgar staginess of his sitters.

While his best portraits, mostly those of acquaintances, suggest a long and careful study of his sitters' characters, his genre scenes owe their success to a rapid "snapshot" technique. Figures are caught in the action of a moment – the coxcomb admiring himself in a glass, the drunkard toppling over, the debauchee ogling, the cat arching its back, the dog sniffing the contents of its master's pocket. Delighted by such incidents, Hogarth sometimes overcrowded his pictures with them to fill out the story and point the moral more forcibly. His details, however minute, are seldom irrelevant. In the fourth scene of *Marriage à la Mode*, *The Levée* (Pl. 27B), the Viscountess, far advanced on the path of fashionable extravagance, sits sipping her coffee as she listens to the endearments of her lover whilst foreign songsters warble and a negro page unpacks a newly acquired collection of *virtu*. Having taken the opportunity of satirizing the cult for antiques, one of the many vices into which the couple has fallen, he has carefully bound this theme to the main action by hanging a picture of Jupiter and Io above the Viscountess and the lawyer, a Ganymede above the *castrato* singer, and by placing a bronze of the horned Acteon in the hands of the grinning page.

Brilliancy of handling, an almost French delight in *matière*, is the quality which distinguishes Hogarth from all his contemporaries, and is evident even in his earliest pictures of a scene from *The Beggar's Opera* of which he executed several versions between 1728 and 1729. The paint is applied *con amore* in rich rococo scrolls and suggests some intimate knowledge of French painting, though how he came by this technique is a mystery. It is seen at its best in the *Marriage à la Mode* series, in several of the intimate portraits and, at its most astonishing, in *The Shrimp Girl* (National Gallery), a virtuoso performance in which delicacy of touch and glancing caressing brush-strokes approach the refinement of a Degas pastel sketch. Unfortunately such happy marriages of hand and eye are rare in his work; there is little of it in the majority of conversations, less in *The Rake's Progress* (Soane Museum) and none whatever in the great canvases with which he so perversely hoped to establish his fame as a history painter.

Portraits. In 1731 George Vertue remarked that Dahl, Richardson and Jervas were the "three foremost old masters"; Kneller had died eight years before and no one had succeeded to his commanding position. Michael Dahl, a Swede, had settled in England in 1689 and, although he continued to paint until 1740, he had done his best work before this period began and long outlived the fashion for his portraits. Of his two chief rivals, Jonathan Richardson is the more interesting and not without historical importance as the pupil of John Riley, and thus the heir to an English tradition. If his heavy-jowled, pompous men and hoydenish women are boring, at least they are so in the beer-sodden, fox-hunting manner of the English squirearchy and not in any affected foreign fashion. "The good sense of the nation is characterized in his portraits," wrote Walpole; "you see he lived in an age when neither enthusiasm nor servility were predominant." Charles Jervas is principally remembered for the portraits of the literary friends with whom he associated, and it is ironical that the sparkling genius both of Swift and of Pope should be represented by such a dunce of an artist. Both Jervas and Richardson had visited Italy and both were fervent admirers of the *seicento*; the former copied old masters, the latter collected their drawings and wrote influential books about them, but neither seems to have learned much from the Italian school, possibly because they lacked humility. Upon finishing a copy of a Titian, Jervas was heard to exclaim, "Poor little Tit! how he would stare." Other portrait painters working in London at the same time included John Vanderbank, who initiated the fashion for dressing female sitters in Rubens costume, and William Aikman, a Scot who moved to London on Kneller's death with the hope, no doubt, of profiting from such a reign of dunces.

It was on this scene of almost "Universal Darkness" that the bright light of Hogarth burst in the late 1720's. But he was not the only representative of a freer, lighter style, for Joseph Highmore emerged at about the same sime. Like Hogarth, he painted with great directness, was sensitive to French influence, which he probably derived from Gravelot, and was most successful in portraits of the middle class from which he sprang (Pl. 26A). He is said to have painted more family pieces than any of his contemporaries, but few have been identified. Bartholomew Dandridge also painted family pieces which play a part in the development of the conversation piece, but most of his ordinary portraits are dreary exercises in the manner of Vanderbank – distinguishable by the long-nosed, sullen faces with which he endowed his sitters.

Fashionable portraiture seems to have been the prerogative of foreign artists, of whom the most interesting was Philip Mercier, who arrived in London in the mid-1720's and was able to give his sitters a mondaine French elegance. For some ten years he enjoyed the patronage of the Prince of Wales and then fell from power; in 1738 he appears in Leicestershire and in 1742 in Yorkshire, where he painted a number of life-sized portraits. In 1737 the artistic dovecotes of London were fluttered by the arrival of a less able but more successful French painter, Jean Baptiste Van Loo, who had already made a reputation for himself in Paris and Turin, and thus arrived with a *cordon bleu* of continental approbation. Without being unduly frenchified, he was a little less dull than Richardson, whose power was on the decline, and he stayed five years enjoying the prosperity of the most fashionable practice, which he shared with two other foreigners, Rusca and Andrea Soldi.

Thomas Hudson, the pupil and son-in-law of Richardson, was the only native painter capable of putting up any effective opposition to this invasion. Principally remembered as the master of Reynolds, he has been praised far above his deserts. Occasionally he excelled himself in female portraiture but he generally appears as little more than a fashionable painter able to essay the "serious and the smirk"; his gentlemen have a solidity and strength occasionally reminiscent of Dahl, but his ladies tend to be too feathery and coy, especially when dressed *à la Hélène Fourment*. In his female portraits the rendering of stiff silks and satins is often felicitous, for which credit is due to the indispensable Van Aken. Another minor artist who attracted a fashionable clientèle was George Knapton, a foundation member of and official painter to the Society of Dilettante. A portrait of Lord Burlington (Pl. 30A) shows his ability to combine the new natural style with an air of grandeur.

In 1739 a young Scottish painter, Allan Ramsay, who had just returned from Italy, settled in London, and within a year he was able to claim, "I have put your Vanloos and Soldis and Roscos to flight and now play the first fiddle myself". He mentioned no English rival, and there was indeed none to compare with him for the sure-handed elegance or delicate sensitivity which he was to refine through the years. As may be seen from the full-length of the great collector Dr Mead, which he presented to the Foundling Hospital in 1746, he had learned enough from baroque portraiture to adapt the style successfully to an English sitter without giving him a foreign air. He had also learned to adapt poses from the antique and painted the twenty-second Chief of MacLeod pacing the strand in the attitude of Apollo Belvedere, thus anticipating the attitude of Reynolds' *Commander Keppel* by five years. As Professor Waterhouse has indicated, "the marriage of the Italian grand style to British portraiture was primarily the achievement of Ramsay". But he was not limited to the grand manner and could with equal facility depict the quiet, the thoughtful and the reticent. Although he made use of a drapery painter – for he could not otherwise have satisfied the number of his sitters – he gave clear instructions on how the work was to be done and was well able to do it himself, as the lovely portrait of his second wife (now in Edinburgh) testifies.[2] In 1755 he visited Rome again and modified his style by contact with Pompeo Batoni, A. R. Mengs and the French pastellists. After his return in 1757

[2] This portrait was painted in Rome where he would not presumably have had the assistance of a drapery painter. *The Connoisseur*, vol. CXXXVII, No. 552, p. 82.

he painted some of his best works, including the portrait of Dr Hunter, but his appointment as Court painter on George III's accession involved him in a tedious routine of official portraiture which robbed the country of a notable artist.

It is probable that Ramsay's second visit to Italy was precipitated by the rising fame of Joshua Reynolds, who had returned thence in 1754. Five years later Walpole wrote, "Mr Reynolds and Mr Ramsay can hardly be rivals; their manners are so different. The former is bold and has a kind of tempestuous colouring, yet with dignity and grace; the latter is all delicacy. Mr Reynolds seldom succeeds in women, Mr Ramsay was formed to paint them." The solidity and forthrightness of Reynolds' style now (see *Admiral Holburne and his son* in the National Maritime Museum, Greenwich) are certainly more masculine than Ramsay's, but he had yet to prove himself the great all-round portrait painter. Working in the provinces during these years and beknown to few, Thomas Gainsborough was developing a style more individual and revolutionary. Untouched by the Mediterranean tradition, he imbibed French influences from Gravelot, under whom he worked for a brief spell. Like Reynolds, he more properly belongs to the classical age of English painting, but before George II had died he had already executed some of his most masterly works, such as the picture of his daughters chasing a butterfly (National Gallery), which has a morning freshness and innocence he was never to recapture.

Conversation pieces. Deep as its origins may lie in the history of European painting, the conversation piece – a small-scale group of figures placed in a more or less informal arrangement – was first developed in England into an independent genre in the first half of the eighteenth century. Philip Mercier seems to have been responsible for the introduction of the genre which he handled with a gallic lightness of touch especially noticeable in his earliest known painting, *Viscount Tyrconnel and his Family* (1725–6, Belton House) and *Frederick Prince of Wales and his Sisters* (National Portrait Gallery). The greatest practitioner of the conversation piece was Hogarth, who contrived to give it a freshness few of his contemporaries achieved, though he rarely succeeded in bridging the gulf between informality and awkwardness. In the 1730's and '40's the younger Marcellus Laroon painted a few and drew more (page 66), in which he made only the most perfunctory attempts at compositional arrangement; his works have the air of being representations of life at its least formal. Gawen Hamilton and Charles Philips paid more attention to composition, perhaps at the cost of naturalness. See Hamilton's *Artists' Club* (National Portrait Gallery); Philips painted thirteen doll-like members of the Finch family in a little picture which also finds room for a crumbling triumphal arch, a bright new Palladian temple, statuary, and a landscaped vista terminating on an obelisk, to exemplify their taste for architecture. The mode was also, though less frequently, employed by

Bartholomew Dandridge, whose most notable contribution is *The Price Family* (Washington).

Most of the artists who painted conversations found the genre too unremunerative, but Arthur Devis clung to it and produced a vast number between the early 1740's and his death in 1787. "His pictures are all of a sort", wrote Lord John Cavendish in 1764; "they are all whole lengths of about two feet long; and the person is always represented in a genteel attitude, either leaning against a pillar, or standing by a flower pot, or leading an Italian greyhound on a string, or in some other such ingenious posture." Genteel his figures certainly are, but they have a melancholy *naïveté* which has endeared them to collectors in recent years. A good and representative example, painted in 1751, shows Sir George and Lady Strickland enjoying the carefully contrived rustic charms of their park.

Fancy pictures. Like the conversation piece, the fancy picture was of French extraction, and was popularized, if not introduced, by Philip Mercier. In a valiant and characteristically confused attempt to define the new form, Vertue said the pictures were "pieces of some figures of conversations as big as life; conceited plaisant fancies and habits; mixed modes really well done – and much approved of". Faber in 1739 engraved nine such works after Mercier, who, profiting from the example of Hogarth, seems to have conceived his pleasant fancies – *A Venetian Girl at a Window*, *A Recruiting Officer* and the like – with an eye to the growing market for prints. The most notable English practitioner of the genre was the versatile Francis Hayman, who began his active career by working with Gravelot on the plates for Sir Thomas Hanmer's edition of Shakespeare which was published in 1744. At the same time Hayman began the large fancy pictures of pastoral and Shakespearean subjects to decorate the boxes of the Vauxhall Pleasure Gardens. These works were strongly tinged with Gravelot's French influence but they remained English in conception and execution. The charm is always a little rustic, the comedy a little heavy-handed, the texture more than a little coarse. Like the pictures painted for reproduction in prints, they were intended to please a predominantly middle-class public. Historically they are of importance as the most frequently seen contemporary paintings in London and because they look forward to the fancy pieces of Gainsborough and the Shakespearean illustrations commissioned by Alderman Boydell. To our eyes they seem little more than cumbrous translations of French comedies into an English dialect.

History painting. A period which begins with Thornhill's commission to decorate the cupola of St Paul's and ends with Hogarth's *Sigismunda* and the first of Gavin Hamilton's vast neo-classical machines might appear to be one of singular importance in the development of history painting. It is, however, very difficult to discern any clear process of evolution. As far as this period is concerned, Sir

James Thornhill is of greater importance as the father-in-law of Hogarth, who derived several ideas from him, than as a decorative artist, for, although he continued active until the late 1720's, and much of his most important work was done in the reign of George I, he belongs stylistically to the previous epoch.

While Thornhill was intriguing for the St Paul's commission, William Kent, a young Yorkshireman, startled the artistic world of Rome in 1713 by winning the Pope's medal for painting. He was even allowed to paint the ceiling of a Roman church, at his own expense. But Kent's early promise to be *Raphael Secundus* was not fulfilled after his return home, and there must have been few besides his devoted patron, Lord Burlington, who could trace in his productions "Titian's strong fire and Guido's softer grace". His mythological ceilings were uncommonly ponderous save in the "grotesque" decoration of their surrounds, and even Lord Burlington modified his opinion as soon as Kent discovered a genuine talent for interior decoration, the designing of furniture and landscape gardening. Much of his popularity as a painter may well have depended on his nationality, and it is not without significance that the first minister, Sir Robert Walpole, chose him to decorate Houghton. Of the few other English artists who indulged the declining taste for painted ceilings, Francis Hayman was probably the most notable.

Thornhill's success at St Paul's seems to have stemmed the invasion of Venetian artists who specialized in decorative histories, though the last of these visitors, Jacopo Amigoni, arrived in 1730 and left in 1739. His series of paintings illustrating the story of Jupiter and Io at Moor Park is with little doubt the most accomplished example of rococo art executed in England (Pl. 30B). Unlike his predecessors, Amigoni painted on canvases which were let into the wall, and he found a satisfactory market for large mythological subjects, though he was finally forced to turn his hand to the remunerative task of portraiture, in which he made unstinted use of the history painter's properties.

When the fashion for large decorative mythological paintings in the house had declined, it may well have seemed that all demand for history pictures was dormant. Generally speaking, the Church neither encouraged nor even welcomed paintings, though Vincenzo Damini executed some of saints in Lincoln Cathedral in 1728, and James Parmentier an altar-piece for Holy Trinity Church, Hull; and there were others of less note. Hogarth, who had aspirations to be a great history painter, solved the problem by presenting large biblical scenes to hospitals. He gave St Bartholomew's Hospital two vast canvases, *The Pool of Bethesda* and *The Good Samaritan*, in 1736, and in 1745 he persuaded three other artists, Hayman, Highmore and the Rev. James Wills, to join him in presenting histories to the Foundling Hospital. This important institution was the first place in London where contemporary paintings might regularly be seen by the general public. No doubt Hogarth's gift was partly activated by his usual desire for self-advertisement, but it appears to have borne fruit in one commission only, the *Paul before*

Felix, which he painted for Lincoln's Inn in 1748. In 1756 he painted a large trip-tych for St Mary Redcliffe, Bristol, and in 1759 the notorious *Sigismunda*, which was in deliberate imitation of a picture by Furini (then believed to be by Cor-reggio) and was greeted with howls of execration, though it might have been received enthusiastically had he passed it off as an old master.

Landscapes. The most important early Georgian landscape painter was John Wootton, who was capable of working in both the current traditions: the topo-graphical based on the Anglo-Dutch painters of the seventeenth century, and the decorative which depended on Claude, Gaspar Poussin and Salvator Rosa. Prob-ably the pupil of Jan Siberechts (with whom he appears to have been working in 1694), he achieved fame as an animal painter; but the topographical aspect of his training is evident in several of his hunting pieces and in a view of Newmarket, in which he devoted no less care to the accurate rendering of the landscape back-grounds than to the horses. Under the patronage of the third Duke of Beaufort, he went to Rome in the early 1720's. His decorative paintings reveal an eye for fine gradations of greens and browns and suggest that his attitude to the works of Gaspar Poussin may have been modified by his knowledge of the parks land-scaped by William Kent. When his work is considered as a whole, he has the best claim to the hotly disputed title of the "father of English landscape". His pupil, George Lambert, was also capable of attractive imitations of the Franco-Italians, but is more notable for the topographical views in which he used his experience as a theatrical scene painter to impose some art on the depiction of the English countryside – as in his views of Chiswick (Pl. 28B).

In 1746 another influence was introduced by the arrival of Canaletto, who had presumably felt the dearth of English grand tourists occasioned by the War of the Austrian Succession. Spending some nine years in England, he painted views of London and a number of English parks all bathed in a mellow or sparkling Venetian light. He attracted the imitation of Samuel Scott, who had hitherto been a marine painter working very ably under the influence of the Van de Veldes (Pl. 29). It is not inappropriate to mention here that marine painting enjoyed a limited popularity throughout the period. One of its most notable exponents was Charles Brooking, who died young in 1759, but had already shown signs of break-ing away from the Van de Velde tradition, which was otherwise predominant.

As the reign of George II drew to its close, two greater English landscape painters emerged, Thomas Gainsborough and Richard Wilson. The former had indeed done much of his best work in this genre before 1760 and as early as 1748 painted the picture known as *Gainsborough's Forest* (National Gallery), welding the elements of the Suffolk countryside into a purely Dutch composition. In the same year he presented his more revolutionary view of the Charterhouse to the Found-ling Hospital – a delightfully fresh treatment of a topographical subject, in which every element is equally important and subordinated to the pictorial intention. He appears in a different light in 1755, at Woburn Abbey, painting two over-mantels of pastoral scenes which are derived, through Gravelot, from France, and anticipate his fancy pictures.

There was nothing revolutionary about the topographical views which Richard Wilson presented to the Foundling Hospital in 1746, but in 1750 he departed on his momentous journey to Italy, where he remained some seven years, absorbing not only the styles of Gaspar and Claude, but the very light and spirit of the Italian scene. In contrast with the artists who merely imitated the Franco-Italian painters, he derived inspiration from them, and never condescended to the execution of pastiches, possibly because he had also been influenced by Dutch art. Like Claude, he invested the Campagna with a melancholy beauty no Italian has ever repre-sented, expressing the nostalgic yearning of the northerner for the south. The pro-spect of *Rome and the Ponte Molle* of 1754 (Pl. 28A) is sufficient to record the advance he made in landscape painting. This lyrically evocative composition is in the manner of Claude, but as distant from him as is *The Castle of Indolence* from *The Faery Queen*: Wilson has, so to speak, employed a Claudean stanza. It is an inde-pendent work of art, neither a mere topographical view nor an insignificant furniture piece.

SCULPTURE

HUGH HONOUR

THE market for sculpture during this period was considerably narrower than that for paintings, and, although it increased slightly, it never spread beyond a relatively small section of the aristocracy. Because of this more exclusive patronage, sculpture remained immune from those social forces which introduced a spirit of naturalism into painting. The isolation was also due to the dominant position held by the trio of foreign sculptors – Rysbrack, Roubiliac and Scheemakers – whose sepulchral monuments adorned with periwigged statesmen, full-skirted ladies, weeping loves, fates, skeletons and angels of doom introduced the last reverberating trumpet notes of the baroque into our cathedrals and churches. But, if the extravagant con-tinental style of these artists was allowed to flourish in church, classical manners were alone tolerated in the private house. The patrician residences of this period might contain a small collection of antique marbles augmented by modern copies of the more famous Roman statues, a few busts and some heavy chimney-pieces in which low-relief carvings were sometimes set. Plaster copies of classical statuary, busts of notable men and terracotta statuettes of monumental figures by Rysbrack and Roubiliac were, of course, cheaper and might be found in the homes of the less affluent *virtuosi*.

Busts. A writer in *The London Tradesman* remarked in 1746 that "the taste for busts and figures prevails much of late years and in some measure interferes with portrait painting. The nobility now affect to have their busts done that way". Whole-length figures in marble were rarely to be met with outside public buildings (amongst the most notable are Roubiliac's *Newton* at Trinity College, Cambridge, and Scheemakers' *Shakespeare* in Westminster Abbey), but the popularity of busts increased apace, partly because three notable sculptors were available to execute them. The first of the foreigners to arrive in England was Michael Rysbrack, who settled in London in 1720 and won an almost immediate success. From the first his busts demonstrated a classicizing tendency, derived from François Duquesnoy through Van der Voort, but although they are often dressed in togas they are not without realism. Even that of George I (Pl. 35A), crowned with laurels and attired in antique armour bearing the insignia of the Garter, is full of strength and character. In treating that most difficult of sculptural problems, the full-bottomed wig, he contrived to make it appear a part, and never an overshadowing part, of the classical composition, as is particularly notable in the bust of Sir Hans Sloane (British Museum). In contrast, Louis François Roubiliac, who settled in London in about 1732, worked solely in the rococo style. Whereas Rysbrack's busts look one calmly, squarely and perhaps coldly in the face, Roubiliac's sometimes give one no more than a glance as the head turns away to assume some character-istic attitude (Pl. 34B). Although cast in a classical mould, Roubiliac's bust of Pope (Pl. 34A) reveals his preoccupation with the mood and appearance of a moment. Peter Scheemakers, who settled in London in about 1730, has usually been relegated to the third place in this group, but he was an artist of no mean ability. His busts are closer in style to those of Rysbrack than Roubiliac (Pl. 35B). Unlike his greater contemporaries, Scheemakers employed assistants to work his marble, and it is significant that nearly all prominent Late Georgian sculptors, including Joseph Nollekens and Thomas Banks, learnt their art in this way.

The fashion for busts was not confined to those of living notabilities, but ex-tended to Roman writers and British poets, philosophers and kings. Roubiliac executed a series of ten marble busts of notable British writers, scientists and scholars for Trinity College, Cambridge, Scheemakers a group of four English poets for Hagley Hall, and Rysbrack seems to have made a speciality of this type of work, carving busts of such diverse figures as Raleigh, Cromwell, King Alfred and Milton. These busts were carefully modelled on such portraits as were avail-able, and the sculptors took great pains to be correct in the details of dress. British worthies were not the only ones to be commemorated and Rysbrack executed busts of Michelangelo, Palladio, Duquesnoy, Rubens and Van Dyck, but they do not appear to have enjoyed the same popularity.

Recent authors might be allowed to stand beside the classics in the library, but living artists could hardly be given a footing amongst the ancients, and the

E

A Concert at Montagu House in 1736, by Marcellus Laroon,
reproduced from a pencil drawing. *British Museum*.

original works of modern sculptors were rarely admitted to the collection of marbles. The copies of Roman statues which filled the niches in the saloon were frequently the work of Italian hands, but towards the end of our period two young British sculptors, Joseph Wilton and Simon Vierpyl, supplied such works for Wentworth Woodhouse, and Vierpyl executed similar figures for Lord Charlemont. Independent works for the house were of a purely decorative nature. Rysbrack, Scheemakers, Delvaux (who worked in England for a short time), Sir Henry Cheere and others were not too high-minded to stoop to the execution of chimney-pieces, many of which were of great size and magnificence, supported on heavily carved consoles, severe terms or buxom caryatids, garlanded with fruits or entwined with vine leaves and surmounted by low-relief panels (which were more frequently in stucco). The low reliefs – such as those that Rysbrack executed for Clandon, Houghton and Woburn Abbey – were predominantly classical in feeling to accord with the pedimented door-cases and other Palladian features. Roubiliac alone seems never to have executed such works, possibly because his rococo style was thought to be unsuitable, though gay Italian stucco work was admitted on walls and ceilings.

Of the few large independent figures executed for private patrons in this period, that of Hercules which Rysbrack carved for Stourhead in 1756 is the most important (Pl. 32). Horace Walpole tells how this athletic statue, which he terms "an exquisite summary of his (Rysbrack's) skill, knowledge and judgement", was modelled on the head of the Farnese Hercules and otherwise "compiled from the various limbs of seven or eight of the strongest and best made men in London, chiefly the bruisers and boxers of the then flourishing amphitheatre for boxing, the sculptor selecting the parts which were most truly formed in each". This figure marks an important stage in the history of English sculpture, for it was commissioned as a statue and not a mere piece of household or garden furniture, it was an original work derived from the antique but modelled on nature and, furthermore, it was placed amongst casts of the most famous Roman statues in the Pantheon at Stourhead. Roubiliac's large figures were nearly all portrait statues, the most important exception being that of *Religion* which he executed for Gopsal in 1761 (Pl. 33); finely and sensitively wrought, like all his works, it is in the tradition of Roman late baroque sculpture and strikingly representative of his *retardataire* tendency. The earliest, and in many ways the best, of his statues was that of Handel, which he executed for the Vauxhall Pleasure Gardens in 1738. It shows the composer rather untidily dressed, having taken off one of his slippers, and sitting back in an easy posture to strum the lyre which, like the *putto* at his feet, strikes an incongruous note in this otherwise realistic work.

LATE GEORGIAN

PAINTING

HUGH HONOUR

"Our eloquence and the glory of our arms have been carried to the highest pitch. The more peaceful arts have in other countries generally attended national glory. If there are any talents among us, this seems the crisis for their appearance: the Throne itself is now the altar of the graces, and whoever sacrifices to them becomingly, is sure that his offerings will be smiled upon by a Prince, who is at once the example and patron of accomplishments" (Horace Walpole in the preface to *The Anecdotes of Painting*, 1760).

It was with such high hopes that the artistic world of London greeted the accession of George III, and, although royal patronage was to fall short of Horace Walpole's expectation, his prophecy was in the main fulfilled. It is sufficient to mention the names of the principal artists of the period to show that it was indeed the golden age of English painting and sculpture—Reynolds, Gainsborough, Wilson, Stubbs and Romney were all at the height of their powers, as were also the water-colourists J. R. Cozens and Thomas Girtin, and the sculptors Wilton, Banks and Nollekens. The first few years of the period were illuminated by the sunset of Hogarth, Thomas Hudson, Allan Ramsay and the trio of anglicized sculptors, Roubiliac, Rysbrack and Scheemakers. The first few years of the nineteenth century saw the rise of Lawrence, Raeburn, Constable, Blake, Turner and Flaxman, who had already begun to make their personalities felt. Indeed, it would not be too much to say that all but a handful of the greatest English artists worked during the long reign of George III.

For the history of English painting, no less than for the painters themselves, the most important event in the period was the foundation of the Royal Academy. Such an institution for the establishment of the "rules" of high art is, of course, a necessary adjunct of any classical period; but the forces which brought about the foundation of the Academy in England were perhaps social as much as artistic, and it reflects the decline of aristocratic patronage and the rise of a much more diffuse and less homogeneous class of patrons. It is unnecessary to repeat here the tedious history of the jealousies and squabbles which marked the earliest years of the Royal Academy. *Tantaene animis caelestibus irae?* Suffice it to say that a group of artists who had exhibited works at the Foundling Hospital held a larger exhibition in the rooms of the Society for the Encouragement of the Arts in 1760. This exhibition was a resounding success and gave rise to three rival bodies: the Free Society of Artists of Great Britain which petered out in 1779, the Society of Artists which was incorporated by Royal charter in 1765 and lasted until 1791, and the Royal Academy itself which was founded in 1768 under the presidency of Reynolds. All three institutions held annual exhibitions but gradually the leading exhibitors deserted from the other societies to the Royal Academy where all the most important painters save Romney were to exhibit at some time. The Royal Academy was largely responsible for raising the status of artists above that of mere tradesmen or craftsmen; its banquets were attended by members of the Royal Family, by diplomatists and politicians – a far cry from the jovial carousings of the old artists' clubs. Its schools gave students a good academic grounding with the opportunity to draw from the nude or from a collection of casts such as had previously been available for study only to those with the *entrée* to houses of great collectors. But, above all, its annual exhibitions gave artists the opportunity of studying each others' works and provided them with a shop window in which to show their performances, thus helping to free them from the old system of patronage and the tyranny of the picture dealer. Whereas the majority of pictures had formerly been painted to fulfil commissions, the Academy, and the other societies, opened up a much wider market enabling artists to exhibit history pictures, fancy scenes or landscapes on the chance of finding a purchaser or attracting sufficient interest to justify the publication of engravings.

Much as the artists complained of lack of patronage, especially for large history pictures, the sheer quantity of paintings, particularly portraits and cabinet pieces, produced during this period, is witness to the demand from new and more modest patrons who sought pictures to complete the furnishing of a small town or country house. So widespread became this demand for "art" that an unprecedented quantity of engravings were produced to satisfy the voracious appetites of those unable to afford the price of an original painting. Engravings had always been bought by collectors, indeed, as Strutt remarked, "almost every man of taste is in some degree a collector of prints", but their importance in the history of English painting has never been justly appreciated. They served as advertisements for the painter, spreading his fame far beyond the country house to the trim villa of the provincial lawyer or prosperous tradesman. Mezzotints, stipple and line engravings of the famous beauties of the day, of notable politicians, of scenes from recent history or of fancy pictures found their way into all but the humblest of homes. Their vogue made the painting of modern histories a profitable business and Benjamin West is said to have made as much as £15,000 out of Woollett's engravings of his *Death of Wolfe*. Indeed, artists such as M. W. Peters and Francis Wheatley must frequently have worked with one eye on the burin very much as novelists of today write with one eye on Hollywood. In this way engravings made it possible for painters to cater for a wider public than that represented by the purchasers of original pictures.

Taste and patronage. Nevertheless, the most eminent painters of the day were working for a clearly defined and limited market and their paintings reflect the taste of their wealthy patrons to the same extent as the great houses that were springing up throughout the country and the furniture that was produced for them. The size of rooms still made large pictures fashionable and whole-length portraits, always favoured in England, were turned out in great quantity. But the chaster style of interior decoration introduced by the Adam brothers limited the art of the purely decorative painter to the small roundels of the ceiling, occasional panels in the wall and, more rarely, views of imaginary architecture, supplied by Biagio Rebecca, Angelica Kauffman and her prolific husband Antonio Zucchi. The titanic gods whose athletic amours had decorated many a wall and ceiling in the earlier part of the century gave place to simpering personifications and pretty prospects of ruins. The Adams were also responsible for the conception of a room as a whole with every part in concert from the ceiling to the carpet and from the chimney-piece to the door knob, and pictures must needs fit into this all-embracing scheme. Great portraits by Reynolds and Gainsborough were designed for the grand salon, fancy pieces for the boudoir, history pictures for the gallery; and it is pertinent to note that when these works are removed from their setting the pictures, no less than the rooms, lose much of their beauty and significance. Similarly, Reynolds' portraits of his literary friends, and Gainsborough's of his musical cronies, were intended for the more modest apartments of the town, and the provincial artist's style was adapted to the requirements of the minor country house, reflecting its greater solidity and less elegant refinement. The period is marked by the existence of some good provincial artists who, like Joseph Wright of Derby, worked mainly for the patronage of their district.

Although, as we have already observed, patronage was by no means confined to members of the upper class, their influence remained predominant none the less. This was the great age of the Grand Tour when every young man of good family was expected to have spent some months in Italy where, under the supervision of some bear-leader or guided by a seldom altruistic cicerone, he made a nodding acquaintance with the arts which stood him in good stead for conversation on his return. His more lowly contemporaries were inclined to ape his pronouncements until, as reported by an anonymous writer of 1775, "even the lowest people tell familiarly of Hannibal Scratchi, Paul Varnish and Raphael Angelo". Painters consequently emulated the styles of the most popular Italians of the sixteenth and seventeenth centuries in both portraits and history pieces, though they seldom impressed the newly returned *macaroni* who, like Sterne's critic, would remark of them that they contained "nothing of the colouring of *Titian*, the expression of *Rubens*, the grace of *Raphael*, the purity of *Dominichino*, the *corregiescity* of *Corregio*, the learning of *Poussin*, the airs of *Guido*, the taste of the *Carrachis* or the grand contour of *Angelo*". It was at such moments that Sir Joshua "shifted his trumpet and only took snuff"; though no one was a more enthusiastic admirer of these artists, and the standard of taste in old masters is nowhere better expressed than in the *Discourses* he delivered each year to the students of the Royal Academy. The Italianized taste of the aristocracy, which was also, of course, the official policy of the Royal Academy throughout this period, is displayed to perfection in Zoffany's *Tribune of the Uffizi* into which he has crammed all those objects and paintings which the patron coveted and the artist emulated.

As the tourist admired only the classical sculptures and old master paintings in Italy, so did the painter. Contemporary foreign artists were generally considered of little account save for Pompeo Batoni, the most elegant and expensive portrait painter in Europe; Canaletto, who had nearly disgraced himself in the eyes of Taste by stepping on English soil; Zuccarelli, who came to England in this period but appears to have retained his Italian integrity, and A. R. Mengs who was more popular for his portraits than his history pictures. Batoni's influence may be discerned in the work of Ramsay, Nathaniel Dance and even to a slight degree of Reynolds himself, but the others made little impression on English painting in this period. The neo-classic style, which may owe as much to the Scottish Gavin Hamilton as to Mengs, found comparatively little favour in these isles. Hamilton did contrive to insinuate some of his vast canvases into otherwise immaculate British houses but he had to make their purchase a condition of sale for classical sculptures and old masters. In sculpture, however, neo-classicism enjoyed uninhibited popularity because it emulated the style of the most admired statuary of the past, directly reflecting the taste of the collector.

Partly by his own inclination, and partly to cater for the taste of his patron, the English artist seeking the best market for his works modelled himself on the masters of the *cinquecento* and the *seicento*. He might also turn to seventeenth-century Dutch painting which was ranked second only to Italian, and it seems likely that Gainsborough, Stubbs and, towards the end of his career, Reynolds, imbibed some inspiration from this quarter. As the reign of George III progressed, however, members of the untravelled middle classes began to grow in importance as patrons, desiring less of the grand manner but greater sentiment and truth to nature as they saw it; consequently small genre pieces and English landscapes became more popular. Whereas the great patron would demand grandiose portraits and, on rare occasions, such history pieces as might be mistaken for old masters in a bad light, the less wealthy wanted more intimate works.

Literary influences. It is not necessary to indulge in elaborate comparisons between the oratory of Burke and the grand portraits of Reynolds, or between Gibbon's attitude to history and the paintings of Copley, to see how the main tendencies in literature were paralleled in the painting of the period. White's *Natural History of Selborne* and Gray's diaries have in their scientific observation of nature an obvious parallel in the animal paintings of Stubbs. The spirit of nationalism, which was an important force in the Gothic Revival, was characterized by an increased interest in the earlier English writers and a growing preference for the native landscape adorned by gothic rather than classical ruins – tastes which are clearly expressed in the history pictures and the landscapes of the day. The popularity of Macpherson's *Ossian* was mainly based on the pleasing supposition that he supplied the want of a British Homer, and he was commemorated in painting and sculpture. Ossian's appeal was also due to a curiously remote cult of the simple life, the ideal, the unspoilt barbarian, the noble savage indeed, who was depicted in his own exotic surroundings by William Hodges and was personified in Omai whom Sir Joshua Reynolds painted on more than one occasion.

Above all, the cult of Sensibility pervaded a period in which Richardson's novels were read with tearful affection – not to mention Sterne's *Sentimental Journey* (1765), Goldsmith's *Vicar of Wakefield* (1766) and, most lachrymose of all, Henry Mackenzie's *Man of Feeling* (1771). Novelists and poets indulged a pleasing melancholy strain and invited the tear over descriptions of descents from greatness to misery, ruins (real or artificial), wild landscapes, children and the short and simple annals of the rustic poor. In an age when weeping was a mark of refinement and a young woman might die from excessive sensibility, it is hardly surprising that the dewy-eyed *Magdalene* of Guido Reni should have been amongst the most popular of pictures. The influence of sensibility on art is to be discerned in many a rugged, gloomy or mellifluously sweet landscape, in views of towering ivy-clad ruins, the resort of moping owls, and in scenes from recent history – the death of Wolfe (Pl. 41B) in the hour of triumph or of Chatham "heart sick for his country's shame" – or in genre pictures of rustic groups which "only nature could have supplied and taste and sensibility selected" (to quote the words of Martin Archer Shee on Gainsborough's *Girl with Pigs*). Even in a picture of a scientific experiment – *The Bird in the Air Pump* – Joseph Wright of Derby introduced figures of children to shed innocent tears. With the notable exception of Stubbs, no successful painters in this period failed to succumb at some time to a literary taste which they no doubt enjoyed as much as their patrons.

Portraiture. Portraiture retained its popularity throughout this period, and although artists were prone to complain of its drudgery few were so high-minded as to despise its rewards. Considered as essential for the decoration of a great house by the aristocracy, and as the first emblems of gentility by the bourgeoisie, portraits might be found in practically every house that contained pictures; and the artists, from Reynolds in London to the now forgotten journeymen in the provinces, worked hard to satisfy an ever-increasing demand. As early as 1759 Reynolds is known to have had some 150 sitters, and Gainsborough painted more than 700 portraits in the course of his career. Much as Reynolds hankered after history, as Gainsborough longed to escape to some remote village where he could settle down to landscape, or as Romney wished to realize the grandiose projects he sketched, all three were most admired and are best remembered as portrait painters.

In 1760 Reynolds was well established in London where his only rival was Allan Ramsay who had recently returned from Rome with a brand-new style based on the French pastellists and Pompeo Batoni. But, although Ramsay painted some of his best portraits during the first nine years of this period, most of his time was consumed by uncongenial, though no doubt remunerative, royal commissions, and in 1769 he retired altogether from the scene. The year 1760 is of singular importance in Reynolds' career, for with the portrait of *The Duchess of Hamilton as Venus* he marked his change from the intimate to the grand manner. In the fond hope of deflecting the taste of his patrons from portraiture to "history" he dressed his female sitters in classical garments, placed them in the attitudes of Michelangelo or Albani and sought to draw the general out of the particular. In his use of "timeless" costume he attracted few followers, though Francis Cotes once surpassed himself and nearly equalled Sir Joshua in this manner (Pl. 39A). After 1765, when Reynolds exhibited the most remorselessly classical of all his portraits – *Lady Bunbury Sacrificing to the Graces* – he seems to have realized that the British public would not be dictated to in such a fashion and he resorted to a less artificial if no less magniloquent style. But he never condescended to the ephemeral dictates of the *modiste* and he was consequently able to portray the fashionable hostess of the moment, like Lady Hertford (Pl. 38A), *en grande tenue* as a beauty of all time. In portraits of men he resorted to fewer devices, for his sharp psychological penetration enabled him to paint into them such strength of character as would transcend the bounds of time. The friend of *literati* rather than painters, he was ideally suited to depict the great men of his age, and he painted them with such force that we can now see them only through his eyes. But Reynolds could descend from his dais, dropping the grand manner and his tone of high seriousness when occasion offered: he could even laugh at his high-flown pretensions, as witness the charming parody of his own grand manner in the portrait of *Master Crewe as Henry VIII* or *Garrick between Tragedy and Comedy*. His range was indeed enormous, much wider than has sometimes been supposed. He was very much more than the "official" portrait painter of his age, and his success in his own day, no less than his enduring fascination, resided in his variety – "Damn him," said Gainsborough, "how various he is." He could adapt his style and composition to depict with equal felicity the robust and vigorous admiral or the elegant and diaphanous *belle*, tender and melting motherhood or hard and glittering urbanity.

In 1774 Thomas Gainsborough moved from Bath to London where he could more effectively challenge Reynolds' position as the leading portrait painter of the day. Never before or since has English society been served by two artists so great and so complementary. Whereas Reynolds was a painter of intellect, Gainsborough was of feeling; Reynolds the master of substance and pose, Gainsborough of fleeting effects of light. Gainsborough's more exquisite, more feminine talent, his delicious creamy paint, his fine draughtsmanship and his transformation scene effects will never lack admirers, especially amongst those who find it difficult to appreciate Reynolds' subtlety. Moreover, Gainsborough could be no less effective than Reynolds in the grand manner as is evinced by the magnificent state portrait of the Duke of Argyll (Pl. 22) in which he has firmly grasped the forceful character of his sitter, presenting an image of great power and solidity which is in no way weakened by his delight in the beauty and variety of the textures of his robes, painted, as always, with the utmost virtuosity, in a shimmering pattern of brilliant flicks and blobs of paint. The strength, weight and solidity of this portrait (dating from 1767) was not often to be recaptured, for Gainsborough gradually succumbed to the fascination of textures and surface effects so that his figures became increasingly wraith-like and insubstantial. Enamoured as he was of silk and satins, Gainsborough rarely forewent the pleasure of painting his sitters' costumes himself; his canvases are therefore seldom marred by the mechanical touch of the "drapery painter" or studio assistant, and every part of his best portraits is from his own hand and of equal artistic merit.

Those who desired neither the elevation of Reynolds nor the shimmering evanescence of Gainsborough might, after 1773, employ George Romney, who was born to be the fashionable portrait painter *par excellence*. He could always be relied upon to produce a good likeness, and sometimes displayed a keen insight into character as in his capital portraits of the young Etonian, Lord Grey (Pl. 37), the disillusioned ageing statesman, Warren Hastings, or the elegant young couple setting out to inspect their estate. Eminently professional, his work generally smells too much of the studio, and even when painting his *femme fatale*, Emma Hart (later Lady Hamilton), he appears thin-blooded and coldly calculating. Despite his charm and accomplishment, it is difficult for us now to understand how the London of 1783 could be of two factions, Reynolds' and Romney's.

Towards the end of his career Romney was rivalled by John Hoppner and William Beechey, both of whom catered for more humdrum sitters and produced portraits which appeal to us now mainly as period pieces. They had a sharp eye for fashion in dress and *toilette* which endowed their female sitters with a certain charm, though they occasionally made them look as if they might at any moment fall prey to excessive sensibility. A more lively note was struck by the arch-realist

J. S. Copley, who painted the sparkling rococo group of *The Three Princesses* (Pl. 39B).

Before leaving the subject of portraiture a word should be said of the pastellists who enjoyed a considerable vogue until the 'nineties, when the most notable, John Russell, who had in his heyday commanded prices as high as Reynolds, was forced to tour the provinces in search of sitters. He executed a vast number of portraits, some of which show a refined sensitivity and all of which are characterized by an admirable respect for his medium. Francis Cotes, William Hoare, Ozias Humphrey and Daniel Gardner were also prominent portraitists in pastel.

John Zoffany. The taste for conversation piece portraits, which was well established before the period began, was given new impetus by the arrival in England of John Zoffany. With his almost photographic technique, which enabled him to reproduce the minutiae of fashionable clothes and interior decoration as if seen through a quiz-glass, he won immediate popularity and went to Florence to paint the *Tribune of the Uffizi* (1772–6). This picture delights us now as an amusing and authoritative epitome of the current taste in pictures no less than as an illustration of the Grand Tour, while his equally delightful painting of Charles Townley amongst his "marbles" affords an intimate view of the *virtuoso* at home. Other artists who worked in this genre included Francis Wheatley and Arthur Devis.

Fancy pictures. Sir Joshua Reynolds found it hard to determine whether Gainsborough had "most excelled in portraits, landscapes or Fancy pictures" but confessed himself to have been captivated by "the interesting simplicity and elegance of his ordinary little beggar children". The first of Gainsborough's fancy pictures to be exhibited appeared in the Academy of 1781 and, although it does not seem to have won the approval of the *cognoscenti*, it made a great impression on the artists. Reynolds later bought his *Girl with Pigs* (1782) and essayed the same style in his *Strawberry Girl* and *Shepherd Boy*. Within a few years the exhibitions were abundantly supplied with little scenes of rustic innocence which made an immediate appeal to the urban middle classes. Of the many artists who worked in this genre, Francis Wheatley was probably the most successful but none was more ruthless than George Morland in his pictures exploiting the nostalgia for a rural society that was already vanishing, for a poverty more picturesque, if no less miserable, than that of the town. The genre scenes of John Opie, the Cornish Wonder, are less densely clouded by the romantic attitude to rustic life, the harsh reality of which he had experienced in person.

Closely connected with fancy pictures, illustrations of scenes from contemporary literature also enjoyed a wide popularity. The most interesting artist in this vein was Joseph Wright of Derby, who extracted incidents from Sterne's *Sentimental Journey*, and from the poems of Hayley, Langhorne and Beattie. Although Wright lived solely in Derby, he exhibited regularly in London and never appears to have lacked patronage for his pictures, or a market for prints after them. The source for one of his more remarkable works, *Miravan Opening the Tomb of his Ancestors* (1772) has never been identified but it takes place in the vault of some neo-classical castle – of Otranto or Udolpho – and is a curious mixture of all the fashionable tendencies of the time. John Hamilton Mortimer also painted pictures of a literary character, but specialized in *banditti* which were thought to challenge comparison with Salvator Rosa. A less gloomy figure, the Rev. Mathew William Peters, painted little pictures of a faintly *risqué* nature, illustrated such passages from Shakespeare as could include simpering femininity; and finally, after he had taken orders, turned to religious paintings in the style of Mengs. He too was widely popularized by stipple engravings and mezzotints.

Landscape. Like fancy pictures, landscapes owed their patronage mainly to the rising middle class who seem to have appreciated them for their content rather than for their truth to nature. Consequently Gainsborough found that he could make his landscapes saleable only by the introduction of figures – on one occasion he copied his pig girl group into the middle distance. His landscapes of this period are characterized by a sweet lyricism, a feeling for gently undulating country and an appearance of naturalism, though many were painted from little arrangements of moss and pebbles in his studio. They are, in fact, subtle evocations of the English scene rather than accurate delineations of it, and it would frequently be hard to identify his trees, let alone his grasses. Nor was Richard Wilson a greater respecter of topography except when engaged in painting the "portrait" of a country house in the Claudean setting of its landscaped park. Too much an artist to resort to a purely topographical technique and too stoical to indulge the tear of sensibility, he fell between the two stools of the accepted landscape tradition. It is significant that his most successful picture showed Niobe in a wild setting of rocks, and that it brought in £2,000 for Woollett the engraver. His views of the English or Welsh scene (Pl. 36A) are carefully composed, flooded with Italian light and exquisitely restrained; but they were hardly calculated to appeal to the man of feeling who wished to indulge sweet melancholy over a ruin or be chilled into a pleasing horror by a mountain. Wilson was too classical, and thus out of tune with his age which allowed him to die in poverty.

George Barrett, a man of sound common sense with an eye for the picturesque possibilities of a real scene, produced just what his patrons wanted, and succeeded as a prose Wilson. Artists like Michelangelo Rooker were able to extract the most from a crumbling ivy-clad ruin, and Thomas Patch could do the same for such an Italian scene as *The Falls of Terni*. The Smith brothers of Chichester adapted the Dutch style to the English landscape and achieved a considerable success, both through their paintings and the prints after them. Towards the end of our period

Julius Caesar Ibbetson showed himself an adept of the sweet pastoral scene or the wild romantic landscape, the ideals of which are clearly expressed in such pictures as *A Phaeton in a Thunderstorm* (Leeds City Art Gallery) in which he made use of every device to accentuate the melodrama – lowering clouds, beetling crags, savage country and a modish vehicle involved in a horrifying incident.

Water colour. No outline of landscape painting in the late eighteenth century would be complete without some mention of those in water colour, a medium particularly well suited to the delicate tonality of the English countryside. Water colours enjoyed popularity first as topographical records and then as independent works of art. One of the leading practitioners of the medium, Paul Sandby, was employed by the equivalent of the Ordnance Survey Department. Francis Towne, who is a discovery of recent years, was known in his own time, if he was known at all, as a meticulous and uninspired painter of country house prospects in oils, but his delicate water colours or tinted drawings, in which mountain scenes were reduced to a series of plane surfaces (Pl. 41A) were representative of a trend in the attitude to landscape. His purely linear method is in contrast to the style of John Robert Cozens whose romantic approach, emphasized by smoky washes which endowed his works with a depth and mystery (Pl. 38B), made an appeal to such men of taste as William Beckford. In 1794 Cozens went out of his mind and was cared for by Dr Thomas Monro, an able amateur draughtsman, the friend of Gainsborough and the patron of Thomas Girtin, J. M. W. Turner and John Varley. Until his early death in 1802, Girtin may well have appeared the most promising of these young artists and his brilliant use of glowing transparent colours prepares us for the mature work of Turner in the nineteenth century, though his attitude to landscape was entirely of his age (Pl. 40A). John Varley occasionally came near him in his large views of Wales, but clung more closely to the topographical tradition.

Animal painting. In the earlier part of the eighteenth century it is hard to separate landscape from sporting painting, for until his death in 1756 John Wootton had been pre-eminent in both genres. His successor, George Stubbs, was primarily a painter of animals, and as such he was considered beyond the pale of the Royal Academy until 1780, when he had distinguished himself by exhibiting history pictures and portrait groups. But although he was neglected by the grand theorists, he seems to have attracted a wide and, no doubt, profitable patronage. By scientific investigation he came to a full understanding of the anatomy not only of the horse but of man, all domestic and some wild animals; his curiosity also led him to study flora and enabled him to paint trees and grasses with accuracy. But his painting was characterized by something more than truth to nature, as may be seen from the subtle pattern of curves he derived from a horse, a man and a dog (Pl. 36B). Moreover, one feels that he painted men and beasts to emphasize the greater magnificence and beauty of the animal. In the history of English art he is an isolated figure, for he founded no school of animal painting and his influence is most notable in the work of Constable and the French romantics.

The nineteenth-century school of sporting and animal painting derives from Sawrey Gilpin, a younger and less able painter than Stubbs, who was also forced to exhibit histories in order to win the recognition of the Academicians. Lacking Stubbs' anatomical knowledge and feeling for supple line, he had a great liveliness and was the formative influence on Ben Marshall and James Ward, whose work was begun before the end of this period but belongs stylistically to the next. Gilpin stands above the general run of sporting painters of the time, notably the Sartorius tribe, whose paintings of Derby and St Leger winners, reproduced in countless prints, graced the walls of the horsier country houses.

History painting. Mention of the history paintings of Stubbs and Gilpin bring us to the form of art which, at some time, seems to have excited the ambition of nearly every artist of importance in this period. The belief that history was a higher form of art than portraiture or landscape had been established earlier in the century, and Reynolds gave it further encouragement in his *Discourses*, though his own eclectic, not to say plagiaristic, works in this vein had little but prestige value. Without the patronage of great institutions or a church (religious paintings are relatively few though more numerous than is commonly supposed) for which they might work on the grand scale, painters set up a wail that the "highest" art languished unappreciated. In fact, most of the histories hung at the Academy appear to have been sold; the more important were widely diffused by engravings and Benjamin West seems to have made a fortune out of painting them.

When West arrived in England in 1763 he settled down to paint portraits and "Poussin size" histories, winning an almost immediate success which brought him to royal notice and patronage. These works were little more than exercises after Gavin Hamilton, whom he had met in Rome; but he created a furore in 1771, when it was still customary to represent the heroic in classical dress, by painting the *Death of Wolfe* (Pl. 41B) in modern costumes, though in no whit relaxing his previous grand manner. The great popular success of this picture marked a turning point in history painting; from thenceforth classical subjects gave way to events from English history represented in the costume of their time. However, except for his abandonment of classical costume, West clung steadfastly to the established rules of the genre – notably by his formal composition, his reliance on poses derived from the old masters and his utter disregard for the known facts of the historical scene depicted. The next, and more important, step in the development of history painting was taken by J. S. Copley whose *Brooke Watson and the Shark* of 1778 broke every known rule in the cause of Truth. Copley followed up his success here by painting the *Death of Major Pierson*, the *Death of Chatham* and the *Repulse of the Floating Batteries off Gibraltar*; all of which drew crowds when they were exhibited and enjoyed popularity as engravings.

Whereas West and Copley made a financial success of history painting, James Barry was less ready to conform to the desires of the time and was consequently a failure. His *chef d'œuvre*, the decoration of the lecture hall in the Royal Society of Arts, is however the most considerable achievement of any British artist in the grand style in the century, and the scene which represents the culmination of the *Progress of Culture* (Pl. 40B) – the foundation of the Society – contains so great a concourse of the notabilities of the day that it may find a place even in a book devoted to the art of the English home. He is now remembered chiefly because of his influence on William Blake who considered him the rival of Raphael and Michelangelo, in which judgement he would have concurred. Another history painter to influence Blake was the Swiss Fuseli. As Professor of Painting at the Royal Academy from 1799 to 1825, he exerted a strong influence on the young painters whose work will be considered in the next chapter. But Fuseli is here important as an illustrator of Shakespeare and was widely known by engravings after the vast canvases which he, together with several other artists, contributed to Alderman Boydell's ambitious scheme for a Shakespeare Gallery.

Rowlandson and Gillray. Prints after the most admired history pictures of the time must frequently have found their way into comparatively humble homes where they might be seen amongst their natural antitheses, the caricatures of Rowlandson, Gillray, the amateur Bunbury and a host of others. Thomas Rowlandson's rollicking rumbustious productions, which call to mind scenes from Smollett, are an effective antidote to any impression of overmastering sensibility in the conduct of life in this period. His drawing of the confused rabble visiting the Academy must be before any writer who deals with the high or the exquisite turns of eighteenth-century taste. Less able as an artist, but more virulent as a satirist, James Gillray is more important in the history of caricature (see page 97). The rival policies of Pitt and Fox, the French wars and the *amours* and eccentricities of the Prince Regent gave him the perfect field for his abilities, and he presented the political and social background of the period in its utmost squalor.

SCULPTURE

HUGH HONOUR

ORIGINAL sculpture remained the prerogative of the wealthy in this period; and the middle-class family who might collect pictures in a small way would seldom encounter sculpture outside the church. The wealthier institutions and the grander houses would usually contain a few marble chimney-pieces and, perhaps, a bust, but figures, groups and low reliefs were reserved for the galleries of the wealthy, and others would have to content themselves with reproductions of original works in pottery, terra-cotta, or artificial stone. It was the invention of Coade stone in 1769 which placed moulded sculpture within the reach of a wide public, and this substance, which was impervious to frost, quickly found its way into the houses and gardens of all the propertied classes.

Large sculptured marble chimney-pieces were going out of fashion at the beginning of this period and it is significant that one of the most notable, that carved between 1762 and 1764 at a cost of £325 for the gallery of Corsham Court, was by Scheemakers, an artist whose career belongs mainly to the first half of the century. A more delicate style of interior decoration, introduced by the Adam brothers, demanded less pompous ornaments, and the groaning caryatids were replaced by trim frames lightly carved in low relief or prettily inlaid with scagliola. Although they were sometimes supplied by the leading practitioners, such works can hardly be described as sculpture. Above the fireplace or elsewhere in the room a decorative feature was occasionally made of a low relief such as that carved by John Deare in 1788 (Pl. 42B).

Deare's relief stands mid-way between decorative and what may be called history sculpture, reflecting the more absurd neo-classical tendencies of the period. It may be doubted, however, whether his contemporaries would have shared our delighted surprise on learning that these elegant Greeks were none other than our own King Edward I and Queen Eleanor, for neo-classicism was a stronger and more durable force in sculpture than in English painting.

Long before this period began sculptors were commissioned to copy the celebrated antique statues in Florence and Rome, and when they were asked to produce more original works they were expected to carve such figures as could barely be distinguished from the fragments ingeniously put together by the Roman dealers. In low reliefs and in small figures, moreover, Thomas Banks, the most notable history sculptor of the period, was able to draw a strong personal style out of the neo-classic mode. In his *Falling Titan* (Pl. 43C) he achieved an effect of such remarkable grandeur that anyone familiar only with the photograph must be astonished to find that the marble itself measures no more than thirty-three inches in height. In *Thetis Dipping the Infant Achilles in the Styx* he was able to achieve a three-dimensional quality, rare indeed in English sculpture.

F

Amongst men of taste the popularity of busts increased considerably during this period, no less for the depiction of the living than for the commemoration of the great dead. No "gentleman's library" was complete without its poets and philosophers, the natural genii of the place. Busts of Pope, Milton, Locke and Newton were produced throughout the period, nor were Homer and Plato forgotten. Wilton carved a bust of Alfred the Great for Lord Radnor (who presented it to University College, Oxford); Bacon began his career with a bust of Ossian and later carved those of Dean Colet for St Paul's School and Inigo Jones for the Carpenters' Hall. Busts of the contemporary great were frequently repeated by their carvers, and Nollekens sold seventy-four replicas of his bust of Pitt at £120 a piece. Furthermore, busts were often incorporated in church monuments, as every reader of Gray's *Elegy* knows.

Most notable sculptors of the period seem to have tried their hands at portraiture, one of the most successful being John Bacon who, according to Cowper,

> Gives more than female heart to stone
> And Chatham's eloquence to marble lips.

But, as in the bust of George III (Pl. 43A), it was a precise imitation of draperies rather than animation of features which distinguished his work. In contrast, Joseph Nollekens, unquestionably the best portrait sculptor of the period, dispensed with or formalized the drapery, did away with the wig where possible and consequently was able to work unhampered in the neo-classic spirit. In portraits of ladies – the most notable is that of the Countess of Yarborough – he managed to perpetuate the beauty and freshness of his models, despite a tendency to make them so prettily sensitive that one expects them to blush at an unmannerly remark. His singularly penetrating busts of men – such as Laurence Sterne, Sir George Savile, Dr Johnson, Charles James Fox – are worthy to stand amongst all but the very best painted portraits of the period. Many other sculptors executed busts of excellent quality, like those of Pope Clement XIV and Gavin Hamilton (Pl. 43B) by Christopher Hewetson, but the majority of these have survived only in funerary monuments.

In this period church monuments grew larger and more numerous than ever before and one has the feeling that his way was indeed obscure whose memory was not graced with a tablet bearing at least an urn. A legion of sculptors and stonemasons laboured to fill our gothic churches with an assemblage of classical figures representing not only the deceased but the Virtues, the Muses, and whoever else might be introduced to lament his death or support his tomb. Nor did sculptors find this work unprofitable – Nollekens charged £100 for the sketch of a monument and Bacon received no less than £6,000 for the memorial to Lord Chatham in Westminster Abbey. Indeed, to satisfy an enormous demand the sculptors were forced to employ an army of assistants and some of them never laid hand to chisel once their success had been established.

The Sculptor

Nollekens carving a Venus, by Thomas Rowlandson.

Monumental sculpture was at this time dominated by neo-classicism, which permitted such delightful incongruities as the figure of Admiral Holmes, in breast-plate and toga, resting his hand upon an unmistakably eighteenth-century cannon, or Sir John and Lady Salusbury, who appear to have strayed out of Addison's *Cato* or some long forgotten classical tragedy. Large monuments gave sculptors the chance to include whole concourses of figures bewailing the subject, but when they worked on a smaller scale they usually had to content themselves with a limited stock of symbols: urns, extinguished torches, wreaths and, if all else failed, what John Bacon called "our old friend the pelican".

In the early years of the nineteenth century no sculptor was more versatile in providing monuments for a wide market than John Flaxman, whose work ranges from the gigantic Nelson memorial in St Paul's Cathedral to numerous little tablets in country churches. Although his classicism had been more thoroughly assimilated than that of any other sculptor of the time, he permitted himself to depart from the strictest rules when the occasion offered. His heroic figure of Nelson is by no means without a touch of naturalism in the head and his charming relief of Dr Warton and his scholars, in Winchester Cathedral, is as fresh and vivid as it is unsentimental. Moreover, he was far better equipped to treat the nude than any previous English sculptor, as may be seen from his figure of Death on Lord Mansfield's monument in St Paul's; but his technique is more of low relief than sculpture in the round. It is significant that he is the only English sculptor to win a measure of European fame, albeit this was due more to his linear illustrations to Homer and Dante than to his carvings.

The beginning of the nineteenth century. This brief survey of late Georgian painting and sculpture comes to its close in 1810, when the future of the arts was regarded with much less hope than it had been fifty years before. For more than a decade, Europe had been closed to the student and the collector, though the needs of the latter were amply supplied (as a result of the Revolutionary Wars) by a greater importation of old master paintings than ever before. Martin Archer Shee complained that the country was "glutted with pictures from the best that genius can boast to the worst that fraud can manufacture; until all the wealth of individuals disposable for objects of virtue has been diverted into channels from which our native arts can derive no benefit". For lack of patronage alone, he argued, English art was sinking into a decline; yet it was from no want of employment that Flaxman and Lawrence were rising to occupy the places of leading sculptor and portrait painter; and, on the other hand, it was from no spectacular acts of munificence that Constable and Turner were to become our greatest landscape painters. As the attitude to art, to nature, to life, was changed by the French Revolution and the subsequent wars, so new artists rose to reflect new tastes. Sensibility gave way to subjective romanticism: the real landscape took the place of the

imaginative or improved; and in painting, no less than in poetry, the visionary
was making his appearance.

Although he belongs to the nineteenth century, William Blake, who styled
himself a visionary, had deep roots in the previous era. The contemporary artists
who most influenced him were Fuseli, Flaxman and Barry, who derived much of
their inspiration from Italy. He was one of the first to dispute the authority of
Reynolds' academic precepts as laid down in the *Discourses*, but was none the less
inspired to borrow postures from Scamozzi and Michelangelo. His poetry, no
less than his painting, showed him to be the fieriest of spirits; and yet he illustrated Blair's *The Grave*, a poem redolent with the distant sensibility of the earlier
eighteenth century. Furthermore, in his study of medieval sculpture and manu-
script illumination he showed himself to be a child of the Gothic Revival. He was
very much of the eighteenth century; and yet looked far beyond it.

REGENCY

PAINTING

BERNARD DENVIR

A FEW days after the publication of the Order in Council appointing him Prince
Regent, the future George IV attended a banquet given by the Royal Academy
at its headquarters in Somerset House. He behaved with noticeable affability,
proposing the toast, "Prosperity to the Fine Arts and the Royal Academy".
The remaining ninety years of the century were to see the ample fulfilment of this
wish, a fact which must be attributed in part at least to the efforts of the extraordinary person who so felicitously voiced it. Constantly attending exhibitions, a
collector of works by old masters – the younger George was an enthusiastic, kindly
patron of contemporary artists. His commissioning of Lawrence to paint the series
of portraits which now adorn the Waterloo Chamber at Windsor Castle was
prompted no doubt by that sense of England's historic grandeur which warmed
many imaginations after the defeat of Napoleon, but he had well-defined, less
official, more personal inclinations. From Wilkie he bought and commissioned on
a lavish scale. He was one of the main supporters of that distinguished animal
painter Ben Marshall (1767–1835), who rivalled, if he did not excel, the masterpieces of the great George Stubbs (1724–1806); and in the very Academy banquet
speech referred to above, he paid "high compliments" to J. M. W. Turner's
Mercury and Herse.

On the walls of Carlton House there hung, beside the old masters, works by
Stubbs, Ben Marshall, and Sawrey Gilpin (1733–1807), whose main contribution
to the art of the *animalier* was the addition of wild, romantic landscapes. There
were also: Gainsborough's *Diana and Actæon*, which had been bought for the Prince
in 1797; six or seven Spanish and Italian scenes by Wilkie, as well as the famous
Blind Man's Buff and *The Penny Wedding*, both of which had been commissioned
by the Prince in 1813; Mulready's *Interior of an English Cottage*, and Sir Joshua
Reynolds' *The Death of Dido*.

The very diversity of these paintings suggests the curious fact that, although in
the social and decorative arts there is a distinct and recognizable "Regency style",
the painting and sculpture of the period are not marked by the same well-defined
characteristics. It is perhaps illogical to expect that it should have been so, for

the evolution of style is in the "fine arts" a slower and more involved process than in the sphere of the decorative arts, where the pressure of social and economic factors compels speedier adaptation to that nexus of influences which we call "fashion". Even more baffling to the historian, however, is the refusal of English art during the period between 1810 and 1830 to allow itself to be coaxed into the category of "romantic". Between the works of Lord Byron and Coleridge there are stylistic affinities which cannot, by any stretch of the imagination, be detected as linking the works of Mulready with those of Constable. The dominant type of portraiture was still founded on the formulae perfected by Lely and Kneller and polished up by reference to the international "grand style". It is significant, however, of the underlying "romantic" temper of the time that Lawrence, its most successful portraitist, offered, as his diploma piece on election to the Royal Academy, an immense and horrific image of Lucifer. This was virtually cribbed from the Swiss Fuseli, who for most of this period was Professor of Painting at the Royal Academy schools, a position from which he exercised a great influence on the outlook of many of the younger generation.

Although it is difficult to impose a stylistic label on the works of those painters and sculptors who flourished during the period of the Regency, a list of the works at Carlton House alone suggests the emergence of the pattern which was to characterize English art throughout the nineteenth century. The popularity of animal paintings, the overwhelming vogue for genre pictures, a tendency to pay lip-service to the iconography of classical art, and a penchant for the exotic provided the main themes upon which exhibitors at the Royal Academy's Summer Exhibitions were to supply variations until well into the twentieth century. When John Hoppner (born 1758) died in January 1810 the vacancy created in the Royal Academy was filled by Augustus Wall Callcott (1779–1844), who had been his pupil. Hoppner had been thought of as the peer and the rival to Reynolds; Callcott's name suggests the Victorian era.

In the decorative arts the period between 1810 and 1830 saw the last great statement of the ideals of the eighteenth century. In the fine arts it saw the establishment of those relationships between art and society which have prevailed ever since. The artists of the twentieth century can look back to Turner, Constable, Blake, and to many others who were at the peak of their powers between 1810 and 1830, as their lineal ancestors. Those of the preceding century belong to the remoter branches of the family tree.

The artist and the public. Artists had always been aware, to varying degrees, of the benefits to be obtained from "puffs" and publicity, but the circumstances of the early part of the nineteenth century demanded of them a more extensive acquaintance with this kind of guile. *The Times*, which had been erratic in the quantity of its art criticism, felt itself in 1818 driven to apologize for the fact that:

If we have not been accustomed to notice in our journal the proceedings of the Royal Academy, and especially its periodical displays of the works of genius, it is not because we are indifferent to the welfare of the Royal Academy, or insensible to its claims, but because our observations have been chiefly directed to objects yet higher in respect to National Importance, the great concerns of civil society, of legislation, trade and commerce.

In other daily or weekly papers there was throughout the period a great increase in the amount of space devoted to the visual arts.

Still more important was the influence of the less frequently issued periodicals, the editors of which must often have been hard pressed for material. William Hazlitt, himself a painter, wrote extensively and inspiringly on art in the *Morning Chronicle*, the *Champion*, the *Examiner*, the *Edinburgh Review*, the *Encyclopædia Britannica*, and other publications. He also produced guides to various art collections and other miscellaneous writings about art. He was one of many, and in addition to this ephemeral literature each year more books about art and about artists were published. Many of these were written by artists and were biographical or autobiographical; others expounded theories of aesthetics or revealed unknown aspects of the art of the past, or of other cultures. The Napoleonic campaigns had focused on Egypt an attention which was largely tinctured with aesthetic preoccupations, and from Italy, Greece, Asia Minor, as well as from Egypt itself, there came a constant flow of antiquities. The most spectacular of these were the Elgin Marbles (removed to the British Museum in 1813) and the sarcophagus of Seti I which was bought by Sir John Soane, the architect, from Giovanni Battista Belzoni in 1824 for £2,000.

Art was "news" to an extent unknown in Britain before, and the aesthetic experience of the nation was sharpened by the increasing ease of foreign travel. The poetry of Byron and Samuel Rogers, no less than the prose of countless others who rushed into print to record their experiences before the Acropolis or the Colosseum, did more than anything else to lift art out of the category of a craft, and establish it as a branch of polite learning.[1] Even more important perhaps was the fact that actual visual experience of works of art was being brought within the reach of thousands. For every single person in Great Britain who had seen a "real" painting in 1720, there must have been at least ten thousand in 1820.[2] A growing sense of national pride had led in 1824 to the opening of the National Gallery, after a long and painful period of gestation. Ten years earlier the Dulwich Gallery had been

---

[1] By the 1820's the guide-books of John Murray, with their fairly exhaustive treatment of the fine arts, had begun to flood the market.

[2] In 1720 the only public exhibitions of pictures were those which took place at auctions and sales. By 1820 there were at least five annual exhibitions of pictures in London, one at the Royal Academy, two at the British Institution (one of contemporary paintings in the winter, one of old masters in the summer) and two of water-colours. Various dealers, such as the enterprising Bullock, not only showed paintings in London, but toured them (e.g., Géricault's *Wreck of the Medusa*) around the British Isles. Large collections brought to the London market for sale (e.g., those of Orléans, De Calonne, Truchsess) were put on public exhibition before being disposed of, and many artists (e.g., Wilkie and Haydon) held what we would now call "one-man exhibitions" of their works. There were also regular public art exhibitions in towns outside London, including Edinburgh, Liverpool, Glasgow, Norwich and Bristol.

made accessible to the public, and though the Soane Museum did not become one, in the formal sense, until the death of its founder in 1837, access to its treasures had never been difficult. The popularity of the British Museum was increased by the disputes about the aesthetic value of the Elgin Marbles, and its importance in the world of art was considerable, since art students were permitted to draw from the antique in its galleries. An interesting record of the new rôle which was played in the world of culture by museums and galleries is provided by John Scarlett Davis (1804–44), whose style was closely allied to that of Bonington. He became a specialist in the painting of the interiors of the Louvre, the Uffizi and other famous art galleries (Pl. 45A).

Of even greater importance, as far as artists themselves were concerned, was the attitude of great collectors, who not only made their treasures available, but were prepared, from time to time, to lend artists certain work for study. Between 1810 and 1830 men such as Sir George Beaumont, the Marquis of Stafford, Dr Monro, Sir John Leicester and many others took a positive view of the functions of patronage, helping and advising their *protégés*, and offering them support on levels other than the merely economic.

Nor should it be forgotten that during the period immediately following the Napoleonic wars, London was rapidly becoming one of the more important centres of the art-selling world. The turmoil which followed the French Revolution broke up many of the great collections of Europe, and a generation of art dealers, more alert, more adventurous and more discriminating than any this country had known, scoured the Continent whenever opportunity offered. Men such as Buchanan, Fagan and the Woodburn brothers brought to London works of art which are still amongst our most important national assets. At the same time too, the reputation of the auctioneers, led by James Christie, ensured that several important collections, notably those of the Duc d'Orléans and of the French politician De Calonne, were sold here. The influence of these movements in the art market was considerable; it is doubtful, for instance, whether Constable would have developed as he did, had it not been for the influx of a great number of works by Claude and other landscape painters between 1800 and 1820.

Contemporary artists could now sell their pictures at open auctions, at their own galleries or exhibitions (as Turner did), at any of the large mixed exhibitions, or at the premises of the ever-increasing number of dealers who were prepared to traffic in the work of the living. Above all, the Royal Academy had become so firmly entrenched that it was now a shop-window, a sounding-board and a market. It was difficult to succeed and impossible to maintain success without its support.

Portraiture. Throughout most of the eighteenth century, artists had been complaining about the necessity of painting portraits when they should have been devoting themselves to the claims of "high art". By 1820 it was becoming apparent that their agitations had succeeded. Portraiture was never to lose its popularity, nor to be displaced as one of the most certain ways of making a large income; but it was never again to hold the near-monopoly of the art market which it had enjoyed in England between 1680 and 1780.

Yet by a curious irony England had produced in Thomas Lawrence, who died in 1830, a portrait painter who reached a European eminence which was only to be rivalled by that of Winterhalter half a century later. The son of an innkeeper, his personality is one of the most baffling in the history of British art. A superb, though occasionally a meretricious technician, handsome, a courtier to his finger-tips, fêted from one end of Europe to the other, he was able to charge for his services prices which even now seem very high. A scholar, and the owner of one of the finest collections of old master drawings ever known, he was harassed by the most atrocious, and largely inexplicable financial difficulties, and his habit of accepting half-fees on commissioning led him to undertake far more works than he could ever finish. If a portrait painter's success is to be measured by the degree to which he satisfies the needs and demands of his clientèle, Lawrence was pre-eminently successful.

His technical innovations were so slight that it is difficult to describe any of the many artists whose works were similar in some ways to his own as followers. The word may be applied to William Owen (1769–1825) and to Richard Rothwell (1800–68). The point was of course that few others were able to contact such influential clients. Sir William Beechey (1753–1839) had owed his success to the support of George III and Queen Charlotte, and his works seems to us now sufficiently embedded in that period to excuse our thinking of him rather as looking back towards Reynolds than forward to Millais and Leighton.

Of the other portraitists of the period Richard Cosway (1742–1821) is, after Lawrence, most typical of the spirit of the Regency. This was due rather to his personal friendship with the Prince of Wales, and to his extravert, even eccentric, social behaviour than to any qualities peculiar to his art. Essentially a miniature painter, his style reflects the brittle elegance which that kind of work implies.

By far the most interesting portraitist of the period apart from Lawrence is the Edinburgh-born Andrew Geddes (1783–1844) who had much to do with the revival of interest in etching, and whose works in every medium which he used are marked by strong personal characteristics. He was one of the many artists of the period who asserted the prominence of Scotland in the artistic history of the period (the Regent himself was partial to tartans and had an ambivalent passion for the Stuarts). More famous than Geddes, and usually described as the rival of Lawrence, was Sir Henry Raeburn (1756–1832), whose work, at first sight anyway more rugged than that of his English contemporaries, suggests at times the influence of Hogarth. On the whole, artists from north of the border tended to look towards Flanders rather than towards Italy for their exemplars.

The subdued richness of colour which marked the works of John Jackson (1778–1831), whose career reflected the patterns of the eighteenth century in that it was based on the patronage of such North country aristocrats as Lord Mulgrave and the Earl of Carlisle, suggested the influence of Rembrandt, and there were similar features to be detected in the work and career of Henry Howard (1769–1847), who was also known for his historical and classical subjects. Few artists confined themselves to the exclusive practice of portraiture; Wilkie, Haydon and Etty, for instance, all produced important portraits, and achieved varying degrees of fame in that genre. Amongst the less exalted, the idea of having one's portrait painted was widely accepted as a social necessity. Certain artists specialized in certain types of sitter. Thomas Phillips (1770–1845) tended to specialize in members of the literary world, whilst Samuel de Wilde (1748–1832) dealt with personalities of the stage.

The success of Henry Edridge (1769–1821), who produced successful tinted portrait drawings, was symptomatic of the wide demand for portrait painters, who by now counted amongst their ranks such female professionals as Margaret Carpenter (1793–1872).

During the years 1810–30 it became evident that there would be no dearth of efficient portrait painters for some time to come, and it would be outside the scope of this work to discuss them all. One may note, however, the names of George Richmond (1809–96), David Scott (1806–49), George Henry Harlow (1787–1819) and Sir William Allan (1782–1850).

The *réclame* of men such as Beau Brummell, with their insistence on sartorial uniformity, ensured that the general tone of portraiture would be a good deal more restrained than it had been in the past. Ideals were domestic rather than official; the parlour table was succeeding the Roman arch; the dress-coat, the toga. Wealth had come to be considered more important than station. As we look at it in retrospect, it is not surprising that the Prince Regent, who was by way of being a sponsor of lost causes, should have preferred himself to be painted in rather spurious armour.

Landscape and water colours. The major hypothesis of all romantic art is that it should be engendered by emotion and feeling. In the late eighteenth century the attempt often resulted in a note of false theatricality, a fact largely due to the absence of a suitable vocabulary and of a suitable medium. Feeling and emotion become stale when they are over-polished. The phenomenal development of water colour provided for painters a solution to this problem.

Between 1810 and 1830 there were still living and flourishing representatives of the older style of water colour. John Smith (1749–1831) had been on the Grand Tour with the Earl of Warwick, and his topographical drawings and paintings were always slightly redolent of Hadrian's Villa, but he lived to become, between

1814 and 1817, President of the Old Water-Colour Society. This had been formed to combat the neglect, real or imagined, which the Royal Academy showed of the medium. John White Abbott (1763–1851) was so entrenched in the older practice of the art that in his copying of the old masters he might have been emulating the earlier activities of a Vertue or a Mrs Beale.

Men such as these were, however, exceptional. The new attitude towards water colour was voiced early in the nineteenth century by Edward Dayes (1763–1804), the teacher of Girtin: "The nearer a drawing (i.e. a water-colour drawing) can be brought to a picture (i.e. an oil painting) the better." Water colour made possible an immediacy of expression and spontaneity of feeling impossible before. It permitted of open-air painting; it cleared from the palette those "chiaroscuro" effects which had led Sir George Beaumont (1753–1827), himself a respectable amateur practitioner in the older styles of landscape art, to suggest that a good painting should be as brown as an old violin. It permitted a new devotion to those topographical and landscape subjects which fascinated the age, and having set off with the desire to emulate the grandeur of oil painting, it had come, by 1830, to impose its own standards on that medium.

So closely had landscape art become interlinked with the discoveries of water-colour painting that it is almost impossible to consider them apart. Our current sensitivity to the charm of Constable's sketches derives very largely from the fact that they are, as it were, water colours in oil. Less expensive than oils, more readily adaptable to the decorative schemes of the medium-sized "villa", water colours introduced a feeling for art into new social regions. There were many less famous than John Ruskin, who discovered the ease of execution and satisfaction of accomplishment which the actual exercise of the art entailed. Foreign scenes, hitherto accessible only to the accomplished traveller, were revealed to those whose previous experience of them had been limited to monochrome engravings. The facile art of Samuel Prout (1783–1852) made the inhabitants of Denmark Hill or Putney as familiar with the Gothic façades of Rouen or Chartres as they were with those of their own parish churches. Prout's vast, widely disseminated output would have been impossible in oils. The necessity to "feel" opened up new fields of observation for artists, and though some followed the tradition of Fuseli and Martin in exploring the realms of the horrific, others achieved this end by more familiar means. The sea appeared for the first time as an important subject, igniting the genius of Turner, and stirring the imaginations of Francia, Bonington, Copley Fielding and George Chambers, to name but a few.

The experience of water colour, whether it was visual or practical, endowed the eye with that kind of artistic honesty which Wordsworth and his literary peers valued so highly. It gave the final blow to the persistence in landscape art of those classical accessories which may be thought of as the graphic equivalents of the Latinized metaphors and similes of Pope and Dryden. It destroyed that sense of theatricality so obvious in the work of an artist such as Philip James de Loutherbourg (1740–1812), who in 1767 had become a member of the French *Académie*. He indeed had some excuse, for, settling in London in 1777, he devoted much of his time and attention to devising elaborate theatrical exhibitions and devices, which influenced his work even when he came to devote his attention to the industrial landscapes of the north.

The development of topographical art gave landscape painters an inclination towards regional fidelities. The Norwich School was one of the main nurseries of genius, and the variable talent of John Varley (1778–1842), whose activities as a teacher forced him into exorbitant mannerisms, was at its best when it contemplated the mountains of Wales. Art clubs flourished in Liverpool, Birmingham and elsewhere. Artists frequently became associated with some particular spot. In 1820, 1821 and 1823 Constable stayed with the Fishers at Salisbury, producing that cycle of views of the great cathedral which forms a contrast to his usual preoccupation with Suffolk.

Such allegiances were noticeable in the work of lesser men. Luke Clennell (1781–1840), a farmer's son, born near Morpeth, became an apprentice of the famous Bewick, and though he came to London in 1805 and eleven years later won a prize for a sketch of *The Life Guards charging at Waterloo*, the roots of his art were, in the best sense of the word, provincial. John Glover (1767–1849), also a farmer's son, from Leicestershire, moved in 1794 to Lichfield, where he taught painting and drawing and made his first essays in oil. He did not reach London till eleven years later, and after some time there, during which he helped to found the Royal Society of British Artists, migrated to Tasmania.

Many of his contemporaries based their reputations on a skilful exploitation of the exotic. George Chinnery (1774–1852), who migrated first, in 1802, to Madras, then to Calcutta in 1807, and finally to Canton and Macao in 1827, produced delightful paintings and drawings of Oriental scenes and subjects which are amongst the more fascinating by-products of English art.

Although such men as Frederick Catherwood were ready to endure endless discomfort depicting the landscape of remote Mexico, most artists found the exotic nearer home. David Roberts (1796–1864) and William James Müller (1812–45) shared a penchant for Spain and the Near East; and it is impossible to enumerate the artists whose views of France, Germany, Switzerland and Italy perpetuated for those who had visited the places the memory of one of the highlights of their lives.

France was in a special position, and it was during this period that the artistic relations between the two countries were at their most cordial. England had come to be looked upon as one of the main progenitors of romanticism, and the *Salon* of 1824 was known as the *Salon des Anglais* because of the impression created by the works of Constable, Bonington and Copley Fielding. The precocious Richard

Parkes Bonington (1802–28), born at Arnold near Nottingham, studied for some time at Calais under Louis Francia (1772–1839), who had spent much of his life in England, and who was to be largely responsible for introducing into French art the lessons of the English water-colour tradition. Later Bonington worked at the Louvre and the Institut de France under Baron Gros. His work, brilliantly lucid, clear and spontaneous, was produced almost entirely in France and dealt with French subjects. He also worked in lithography and, after 1824, in oils. Anthony Vandyke Copley Fielding (1787–1855) was, as his names suggest, the son of an artist; and he achieved great popularity in his own lifetime, though he is now less highly esteemed.

The main developments of water-colour painting had been made possible by the work of men who almost entirely specialized in that medium. Peter de Wint (1784–1849), who was of Dutch extraction, is mainly responsible for an immense widening of the visual and technical horizons of water colour, for a startling vindication of its powers of expressing mass and volume, and for his expressionist freedom of handling and technique.

John Sell Cotman (1782–1842) was born in Norwich, and was for some time an employee of Ackermann. His greatest works were connected with the landscapes of Wales, Yorkshire and Norfolk. From 1810 to 1824 he was much preoccupied with the exhibitions and activities of the Norwich Society of Artists, and with producing illustrations for various archaeological books. After various tours in France, he was appointed in 1834 Professor of Drawing at King's College.

John Crome (1768–1821), known as "Old Crome", was also a native and resident of Norwich, who painted in both oil and water colour, bringing to the delineation of landscape and architectural subjects a bold simplicity of handling and sensitivity to atmosphere.

It seems absurd to think of Turner and Constable as "artists of the Regency", yet that fact alone suggests how remote from the accepted pattern of the times painting in effect was. Between 1810 and 1830 both these artists produced some of their greatest works. But though we think of them in the same breath, their contemporaries did not. In 1810 Turner, who was thirty-five, was a popular and well-established artist, and on 17th August of that year he held £7,216, 16s. 2d. in the funds. The critics and the general public saw nothing difficult in his works, and Hazlitt's earlier description of them as "containing the very elements" was a formula which won fairly widespread acceptance. During this period he was consolidating his gains, establishing his reputation, and making possible those post-1830 forays into fields of expression where few of his contemporaries could follow him.

Constable, a year younger than Turner, at the beginning of the period, had yet to become an Associate of the Royal Academy, and at the end of it had just managed to attain that full membership which he was to enjoy only for seven years more. The French critic Charles Nodier had hailed *The Haywain* (1821) as a painting which could compare with the finest of the works of the old masters, but Constable's English contemporaries were obsessed with the "coarseness" of his handling and saw him merely as a minor landscape artist, precluded from greater successes by a lack of technical expertize. Yet during these twenty years he produced, amongst other works, *Dedham Vale* (1811), *Boat Building* (1815), *Hampstead Heath* (1827), *The Leaping Horse* (1825), and the Salisbury Cathedral cycle (1821–4).

In style David Cox (1783–1859), though not of the same stature, merits comparison with Constable. He greatly enriched the technique of water-colour painting, producing by means of wet colours and broken tints a richness and complexity which allowed the medium to assume the textural intricacy of oil painting in the expressionist tradition.

SCULPTURE

BERNARD DENVIR

"Of all the arts," said Théophile Gautier, "the one which least lends itself to the expression of the romantic ideal is sculpture, which seems to have received its definitive form from antiquity." The history of that art in England bears witness to his words. At one point in the nineteenth century there were few forms of life, from "what-nots" to prayer-book covers, untouched by the Gothic Revival. Architects were prepared to cut each others' throats over the respective merits of the round and pointed arch; painters grew agitated as to whether Raphael marked the beginning or the end of artistic excellence. The major problem which exercised sculptors, however, was whether trousers were to be preferred to togas. Works of art in stone and marble enjoyed a comparative freedom from the social exigencies of the time and, though the nude was looked upon as a medium for the indulgence of the baser passions, young men and women frozen into permanent poses exposed their chiselled forms to view in the most public places, without exciting anything but aesthetic comment.

Sculpture, indeed, retained many of the characteristics of the eighteenth century. By its very nature the profession tended to exclude amateurs, demanding of its practitioners an almost menial skill. Men such as Gibson and Chantrey came from lower-class backgrounds; they began their careers as apprentices, and it was not unusual for a sculptor such as John Bacon to "inherit" his father's practice.

Patronage was ample, finding its fullest deployment in the commemoration of political and military achievements, in funerary monuments, and, of course, in portraiture. The practitioners of sculpture ranged from wax-modellers such as the

Mrs Humphrey's print-shop in St James's Street. From a print by Gillray dated 1808.

famous Catherine Andras, who modelled the funeral effigy of Nelson, to national figures of the stature of Chantrey. One may note, as typical of the general run, the names of Matthew Cotes Wyatt (1777–1862) and George Garrard (1760–1826). More successful than either of these was William Behnes (1795–1864), the son of a Hanoverian piano-tuner, and the unlikely preceptor of G. F. Watts. Commanding the ability to display a Roman verism in his portraiture, Behnes was also a draughtsman of very considerable powers.

The poet reads his works. From a drawing
by Henry Moses, *Modern Costume*, 1823.

John Bacon (1777–1850) began as a precocious youth, winning the Royal Academy's silver medal at the age of sixteen and its gold medal a year later, but his subsequent career did not quite live up to this promising beginning. A more interesting figure is that of Samuel Joseph (1795–1850), whose seated figure of Samuel Whitbread is a remarkable creation.

By constant application to the demands of those who indulged in the current passion for the trappings of death, Richard Westmacott (1775–1856) did better for himself than his father had done as a painter, and won a knighthood in the process. He was responsible for the statue of Achilles in Hyde Park, made out of French guns captured at Waterloo, and commissioned in 1826 by the Women of Britain to commemorate the achievements of the Duke of Wellington.

Sir Francis Legatt Chantrey (1781–1841) first achieved fame by his portrait bust of Horne Tooke, the famous radical and scholar, and by an emotionally expressive monument in Lichfield Cathedral based on a design by Stothard. Starting off as a jack-of-all-trades, prepared to turn his hand to anything from portrait painting to woodwork, Chantrey died worth £105,000 as a result of applying to his art many of the principles which were winning acceptance in the fields of industry and commerce. He was the supreme exponent of the pictorial in sculpture.

It was to the studios of Canova and Thorwaldsen rather than to the workshops of ancient Greece that most sculptors directed their attention. There were always sculptors of Italian birth or descent working in England as assistants or independent artists, amongst whom were Pietro Cingolnelli (1760–1825), one of Flaxman's assistants, and John Charles Felix Rossi (1762–1839), the son of an Italian doctor who practised in Nottingham. Rossi was apprenticed to G. B. Locatelli in London, and became an R.A. in 1802.

The peak of the Romanizing tendencies – and one must not forget that in the background hovered the slightly sententious figures of Mengs and Winckelmann – was John Gibson (1790–1866), the son of a market-gardener of Conway, who was apprenticed to a monumental mason in Liverpool. He attracted the attention of that fascinating banker, collector and scholar William Roscoe (1753–1831), and eventually made his way to Rome, where he worked with Canova and Thorwaldsen, and built up an almost mystic reputation for himself. Although Gibson, whose work is to be seen in abundance in the gallery devoted to it at the Royal Academy, was mostly known for his "high art", posterity tends to look with a more favourable eye at his portraits.

EARLY VICTORIAN

PAINTING

JOHN WOODWARD

Portraiture. King George IV died in 1830, surviving by only a few months the painter who had served him so well as Regent and King. Sir Thomas Lawrence had created not only a splendid visual image of his master, but had brought to a superb and fitting climax the lifelong passion of George IV for surrounding himself with the portraits of the men of action of his day. The journeys undertaken in Europe to paint the portraits of those persons who had helped to bring about the ultimate overthrow of Napoleon, which were destined for the Waterloo Chamber at Windsor, had added to the reputation of Lawrence himself, and had also brought about an entirely new respect for English art. But although the influence of Lawrence continued to be noticeable for some years, taste was changing towards a more solid and domestic type of portraiture, consistent with the changing style of costume and the return to a more domestic way of life. The sparkle, "chic", and soulful sensitivity of Lawrence's men and women were alien to the Victorian drawing-room, bearing as they did something of the lightness of behaviour of their times.

The new King, William IV, turned wisely to Sir David Wilkie for his first official likeness, and the result was one of the most imposing, but neglected, portraits produced by an artist in the nineteenth century (Pl. 52). Wilkie's earliest portraits, such as the *Mr Morrison and Miss Bethune* (1805), were painted very much in the Raeburn tradition of solidarity and truth of character, but they lacked subtlety. His fellow Scotsman Andrew Geddes in his early *Self-portrait*, or in the portraits of his mother, is far more arresting and sympathetic. Wilkie, however, found his true *métier* in small cabinet portraits which were among his greatest achievements, and which come as a welcome relief from the acres of canvas used for vapid and stiff full-lengths which the less-gifted fashionable painters have left us. These small paintings vary from crowded conversation pieces such as the *Neave Family* (1810) to his undoubted masterpiece, *The Duke of York* (1823, National Portrait Gallery). His only competitor in this genre is perhaps Geddes, who painted the exquisite small portrait of Wilkie himself leaning on a chair. By 1830 Wilkie had abandoned these small-scale portraits and embarked on the grand full-lengths inspired by his continental travels. They were thought to be Spanish, but were, in fact, much more in the style of Lawrence, worked with the palette of Rembrandt and with reminiscences of the swirl and dash of Rubens. Unfortunately, many of these have been eaten away by bitumen, but those that remain – *George IV* (Apsley House), *Duke of Sussex* (Buckingham Palace) and *The Earl of Kellie* (Cupar Town Hall, Fife) – are extremely impressive in colour and pose and have a solidarity of stance and cast of countenance that is reminiscent of the full-length figures in Holbein's Whitehall fresco. The full-length of William IV is the most remarkable achievement of Wilkie as a portrait painter. He has chosen to represent the Sailor King in the uniform of the Grenadier Guards, using his "Rembrandt–Rubens" manner with strong lighting contrasts and thick creamy paint. The painting of the cock's feathers of the hat is in itself a fine passage of still-life. It is hard now to understand why one critic found it "stiff and starched as any drill Sergeant, glittering with varnish". It is stark, and curiously still, in comparison with the sumptuous, restless, Coronation portrait of George IV by Lawrence, but it matches it in dignity, never allowing the pale face of the old King to be swamped by the scarlet of his uniform. Sir Martin Archer Shee, who succeeded Lawrence as President of the Royal Academy, was a far better man of affairs than he was portrait painter; and his work is consistent but seldom inspiring, and never reached the efficiency and breadth of his successor, Sir Francis Grant.

Younger painters, trained abroad and influenced more by continental academic portraits than by Lawrence, dominated the early years of Queen Victoria's reign, and she herself had no doubts, as she confided to her diary, that George Hayter was the best portrait painter living. Hayter had gone to Italy to study when a very young man, and had there produced some sensitive drawings of his family and of Italian life, whilst harbouring ambitions to be a history painter. On his return to England he quickly built up a lucrative practice, but his matrimonial troubles, although known and condoned by the Queen, kept him outside the Royal Academy. He was never a very gifted painter, alternating between lyrical but rather insubstantial full-length portraits and rather sombre and solemn half-lengths. None the less, he rose far higher than could reasonably be expected in his State portrait of Queen Victoria, seated, crowned and holding the sceptre (National Portrait Gallery), a portrait so well known that its merits are sometimes overlooked, and perhaps the most endearing State portrait of an English monarch that we have. Youth, dignity and ease are all suggested, and it blazed out, with its powerful colouring, amongst the portraits of black-coated statesmen who surround it in the Portrait Gallery. The extent of Hayter's achievement can be seen in the abysmal failures of Wilkie and Archer Shee to rise to the occasion in their own portraits of the Queen. It is not without significance that the Queen commissioned a portrait of Lord Melbourne from Hayter, as she so strongly disliked the "daub" by Lawrence. Melbourne himself, so the Queen records in her diary, had no doubt that C. R. Leslie was the best portrait painter of the day. In the 'forties Hayter, after a railway accident and a disagreement with the Prince Consort, gradually began to fall from favour, and, as his star waned, royal patronage fell on F. X. Winterhalter, a painter of charm, from the Black Forest, whose earliest work in England is attractive but a little spoiled by some coarse painting; but he left a series of paintings without which our understanding of the Queen, her family and her Court would be considerably less than it is. Winterhalter worked in all the principal European capitals, and it is to his credit that all his sitters so completely belong to their own country. There is no attempt to place a Tuileries Second Empire gloss over Buckingham Palace or the Hofburg. His grandest English portraits are *The Duchess of Sutherland* (The Duke of Sutherland), and *The Duke of Beaufort* (Badminton, Gloucestershire). Hayter spent much time composing vast group assemblages which are, despite their overwhelming mass portraiture, extremely able. The first of these, *The Trial of Queen Caroline* (1823, National Portrait Gallery), contained 186 portraits, and his last, *The House of Commons* (1833, National Portrait Gallery), had 375 portraits. This labour, seemingly of love, made enormous demands on his time and energy, but the portrait-head sketches made for the finished pictures are amongst his best work, free in handling and clear in colouring (Pl. 51B). There was a demand for such assembly pieces during the whole century, and many of the commissions came from the Queen. C. R. Leslie, John Phillip, E. M. Ward, and W. P. Frith were all employed in this way; but although their standard was high none of them excelled Hayter. The style was to deteriorate into what may be called "Guildhall Processional".

Some of the most pleasing portraits were those emanating from painters whose main work was not primarily concerned with portraiture. Sir Edwin Landseer must be considered first both for his charming conversation pieces, with or without animals, and for his single figure portraits. Queen Victoria made constant use of his brush for depicting herself, her Consort, the royal children, and the royal pets. When the painter died, she recorded in her diary that she had "thirty-nine oil paintings of his, sixteen chalk drawings (framed), two frescoes, and many sketches". These works include the well-known conversation piece with dead game, which depicts the Queen, the Prince and their eldest child in a room at Windsor, whilst visible through the window is the old Duchess of Kent being propelled through the gardens in her bath chair; the sketch for this is at Kensington Palace. That the painter had a nice sense of humour is evident from the small portrait of Princess Victoire de Nemours, the Queen's Coburg cousin, where the juxtaposition of the lady's hair and the dog's ears cannot be entirely accidental (Kensington Palace). A perfect gift for the painter was *Van Ambrugh and his Animals*, which allowed him one human and a great variety of animal life (Pl. 54A).

The family portraits belonging to the Duke of Abercorn and the unfinished *John Gibson* (Royal Academy) show him at his best as a straightforward recorder of the human face. Sir Charles Eastlake painted a few portraits, and amongst these one of great charm and brilliance of colour of Mrs Bellenden Kerr as an Italian Contadina (Pl. 61A); but as Lady Eastlake remarked: "These 'fancy portraits' as they were called were greatly admired, and would have filled his hands with this class of occupation, had he not pertinaciously refused to devote himself to portraiture." William Etty also produced several portraits of his family and friends of great strength of perception, an example being *James Atkinson* (Pl. 51A). Daniel Maclise rose to dramatic heights in at least two portraits, *Macready as Werner* (Victoria and Albert Museum) and *Lord Lytton* (Knebworth). John Linnell painted on a smaller scale some portraits of extreme delicacy, which are sometimes marred by a rather woolly application of paint; but his portrait drawings of Blake (Fitzwilliam Museum, Cambridge) are masterpieces. George Richmond was a competent craftsman, but his more delicate painting and drawing (often in silver-point) tend to be overweighted, in any assessment of his work, by his full-size, competent, historically important, but deadly dull drawings of heads done in black chalk heightened with white. His self-portraits in the Birmingham Art Gallery and the Uffizi seem to have been influenced by Raphael and the German Nazarene painters. One of the most splendid portrait drawings of the period is the *Self-portrait* by Samuel Palmer (Ashmolean Museum, Oxford), where the painter has boldly projected his features and managed to convey the short-sightedness of his natural vision.

Those artists who formed or are connected with the Pre-Raphaelite Brotherhood between 1848 and 1862 all painted remarkable portraits, but thereafter their taste and skill deteriorated in a marked fashion, degenerating either into extreme affectation or into the realms of "pot-boiling". J. E. Millais is the most obvious case in point if one compares the sparkling jewel-like portraits of *James Wyatt and his Grand-daughter* (1849) and its companion, or the stern authority of *Ruskin at Glenfinlas* (1854), with the weakly painted academical likenesses of his later years. D. G. Rossetti left a touching and perpetual record of Elizabeth Siddal in the hundreds of delicate studies he made of her during their life together (Pl. 59). Her death in 1862 – a date which makes such a convenient dividing line in the study of the Brotherhood's work – caused the features of Jane Morris and professional models to dominate his later work, which is on a larger and coarser scale. Holman Hunt also, in his youthful self-portraits and in his *Canon Jenkins* (Jesus College, Oxford), showed an intimacy and spontaneity which later left him entirely, though his portrait of Wentworth Monk (Ottawa) has a direct and rather alarming impact. Madox Brown painted few portraits but his self-portrait, which so exactly mirrors his character as it is known to us, and his studies of his wife Emma make one regret that he did not turn his talents in this direction more often. One of the most hauntingly romantic portraits of this period is that of Swinburne by William Bell Scott (Balliol College, Oxford), where the small red-haired poet is posed against a part of the Northumbrian coast.

Lord Leighton in 1853 painted oval companion portraits of himself and his sister, Mrs Sutherland Orr, which clearly mirror his continental training and his knowledge of the Nazarenes in Germany. G. F. Watts, whose main work lies outside the boundary of 1860, painted some of his best portraits when he was in Florence as the guest of Lord Holland in the 'forties and in his first years at Little Holland House. These include the studies of Lady Holland (Buckingham Palace and Compton), the full length of Augusta, Lady Castletown (1846, Tate Gallery – Pl. 53), an immature but ambitious attempt at grand portraiture, and the *Sir Anthony Panizzi* and *Princess Lieven* (both in the collection of the Earl of Ilchester). One of his most remarkable portraits is *Lady Margaret Beaumont and her Daughter*, painted in 1862, a work redolent of the era and strangely "Gothick" in its pose and treatment.

The portrait painter had a constant patronage through the early nineteenth century not only from the Court and the aristocracy but also from the middle classes, whose wealth and social standing were being steadily consolidated. Many portraits were painted as deliberate bait for the visitors to the Royal Academy, and there was a steady flow of orders from civic authorities, institutions and colleges for the likenesses of their distinguished members and alumni. The sombre and solid worth of the majority of these likenesses is intensified by the dark clothes of the men, usually posed against dark backgrounds, and later by the fashion for wearing a beard, which was no less of a handicap to a painter than the wig had been to those of the later seventeenth century. Occasionally a painter could enliven his dark palette by a glittering fob or watch-chain. With women and with children it was easier to achieve a gayer colour scheme and a lighter background, but first the spaniel-ear arrangement of ringlets followed by the very severe arrangement of the hair smoothly across the head made the painter's task a heavy one. This severity of dress and hairdressing for both men and women has had a corresponding effect on the judgement of posterity on portraits painted between 1830 and 1860.

Historical painting. Thackeray had some wise remarks to make on the state of historical painting in England when, under the name of Michelangelo Titmarsh, in 1842 he wrote of the painters:

They wisely, I think, avoid those great historical "parades" which cover so much space in the Louvre. A young man has sometimes a fit of what is called "historical painting"; comes out with a great canvas, disposed in the regular six-feet heroical order; and having probably half ruined himself in the painting of his piece, which nobody (let us be thankful for it!) buys, curses the decayed state of taste in the country, and falls to portrait-painting, or takes small natural subjects, in which the world can sympathize, and with which he is best able to grapple.

In the following year he said much the same thing:

They do not aim at such great subjects as heretofore, or at subjects which the world is pleased to call great, viz., tales from Hume or Gibbon or royal personages under various circumstances of battle, murder, and sudden death. Lemprière too is justly neglected, and Milton has quite given place to *Gil Blas* and *The Vicar of Wakefield*. The heroic, and peace be with it! has been deposed; and our artists, in place, cultivate the pathetic and the familiar.

Certainly the old historical themes were dying out and the proud titles such as *Edward the Confessor Spoiling his Mother* or *Scenes from the Life of Elizabeth Woodville*, which figure so frequently in the earlier catalogues of the Royal Academy, were no longer tempting painters. Vanishing too were the heroic allegorical subjects summed up again by Thackeray as *Britannia, Guarded by Religion and Neptune, Welcoming General Tomkins in the Temple of Glory*. The majority of visitors to the Royal Academy were intelligent and well-read families, who spent a good many of their quiet domestic evenings reading aloud to each other from history and from fiction. They therefore studied critically the attempts of painters to bring to life the people and scenes familiar to them from the written word. It was not a coincidence that the *Vicar of Wakefield* found so many painters eager to render the ever-popular episodes.

History painting during the period 1830–60 can be divided roughly into five main groups.

1. *The Grand Style*. This had fewer devotees than in the previous fifty years, but the teaching and inspiration of Reynolds lingered on in a few minds; and the irrepressible Benjamin Robert Haydon was always at hand to preach the cause of grand art and to cover acres of canvas, inspired by those "perpetual urgings to future greatness", with what must be admitted were rather arid results. His most engaging works are the *Cassandra* and *Venus and Anchises* (S. A. Oliver Esq.), which have recently reappeared. It could be argued that Haydon has done a great disservice to the study of history paintings by being such an essential and key figure in its structure. We know so much of his hopes and failures and "the hum of mighty workings" from his own writings that in assessing first the tragedy and then his disappointing canvases there is a tendency to ignore all the other painters who were working in the same vein.

The decoration of the New Palace of Westminster, which arose after the disastrous fire of 1834, led to grandiose schemes which were to engage many painters between 1841 and 1863. There were those who admired the frescoes of the German painter Peter Von Cornelius, but rather deplored the system of the "master mind" and pupils which it entailed. Eastlake urged that the frescoes of Raphael should be followed rather than German Christian art. Lady Eastlake, his remarkable and intelligent consort, had found Cornelius' work extremely boring: "He is the great gun of German Art, and a mere pop-gun in reality: covers miles of cartoon with what are called grand historical compositions, and which consist of an endless repetition of ill-drawn figures of the largest size and the smallest interest." Prince Albert was made President of a commission to study the scheme for decoration, and Eastlake was the secretary. A competition was announced for cartoon drawings illustrating subjects from British history, or from the works of Spenser, Shakespeare or Milton. Haydon, to whom the whole idea was so dear, failed to gain one of the premiums. The final decorations are disappointing, but the works of William Dyce, A. C. Cope and Daniel Maclise merit more attention than they are usually allotted. The two major works of this scheme are the great frescoes by Daniel Maclise in the Royal Gallery, *The Death of Nelson* (detail, Pl. 54B) and *The Meeting of Wellington and Blücher*. Time and central heating have blackened these works, but the scenes of carnage which surround his central groups are indicative of his ability to draw and compose. The end of the commission saw the end of the desire for a national school of history painting, and the new generation of painters moved out of the medieval or early Christian world into the sumptuous marble surroundings of Greece and Rome as conjured up from the brushes of Lord Leighton, Sir Lawrence Alma Tadema and Albert Moore.

One or two painters of the Grand Style deserve a passing reference, and in particular David Scott, from Edinburgh, who worked on a gigantic scale and studied the old masters. Unlike Haydon, he travelled abroad and assimilated something of Delacroix and Géricault from France, as can be seen in his *Philoctetes Left on the Island of Lemnos* (Pl. 55A) and the German Nazarene style in his *Vintager*. On a smaller scale he painted one of the best Victorian history pictures, *The Traitors' Gate*. All of these are in the National Gallery of Scotland in Edinburgh.

Another neglected but historically important figure is Edward Armitage, a student under Paul Delaroche in Paris; he was also the winner of one of the premiums for the Palace of Westminster decoration. After visiting Rome he began to exhibit battle-scenes and history pieces. But it is his biblical subjects, many admittedly painted after 1860, which are his chief monument. Rather statuesque in quality, but filled with glowing rich colour, they make an imposing impact on the spectator. The best of these paintings are *Samson, But the Philistines Took Him* (Pl. 55B) and *Esther's Banquet* (1865) which was his R.A. Diploma work. Paul Falconer Poole was another ambitious composer of historical groups, but at times he almost caricatures the style and shows all the dangers that lay in wait for a painter of mediocre talents. His *Solomon Eagle* is an excellent example of history getting out of hand and verging on the ridiculous. *The Visitation of Syon Nunnery* is a better venture in this vein, but his best work is probably *The Death of Cordelia* (Victoria and Albert Museum).

2. *The Medieval Style*. This term is only a very general one to cover the Early Victorian interest in the period of English history stretching from Harold to the death of Edward III. It is sometimes called *style troubadour*. This same interest can be seen in the vast tournament which was held in the grounds of the Earl of

Eglington's castle in Ayrshire in 1839, a magnificent spectacle, somewhat spoilt by rain, and there are commemorative portraits by Francis Grant and Edwin Landseer of participants wearing armour. Later, a Court fancy-dress ball was held at Buckingham Palace with the Queen as Queen Philippa and Prince Albert as Edward III, and Landseer painted a double portrait to commemorate it (Buckingham Palace). Eastlake made several sorties from his beloved Italy into this period of history, and one of his most remarkable achievements is a painting full of his knowledge of the Venetian School, *The Champion* (Birmingham), which shows a knight in armour and a helmet having a favour tied to his arm by a lady who might have been painted by Paris Bordone. Maclise was also a successful exponent of a style which was to reach its climax in Landseer's *Chevy Chase* (Birmingham) and *Scene in the Olden Time at Bolton Abbey*. Henry Perronet Briggs is remembered now mainly as a portrait painter, but his historical works should give him a more solid position if such works as *First Conference between the Spaniards and Peruvians* (Tate, Pl. 56B) and *The Challenge of Rodomont to Ruggiero* (Birmingham) are taken into consideration. This medieval style has dug deeply into the visual impressions of history not only because of the engravings which appeared in innumerable nineteenth- or early twentieth-century history books, but also for the influence it has had on the stage and on film companies.

3. *Biblical*. Apart from essays of Haydon, Maclise and Armitage, and, later in the century, Solomon J. Solomon, in grand biblical painting, a new attitude was apparent. Wilkie, on the eve of his journey to the Holy Land, explained to his nephew his enthusiasm for the immense advantage he might derive from painting upon holy land, on the very ground on which the event he was to embody had actually occurred. One of his last works was a small painting of *Christ before Pilate*, and it may well be indicative of the work he would have done if he had lived longer. This doctrine of geographical accuracy was taken to its farthest point by Holman Hunt. William Dyce, inspired both by Raphael and the German Nazarene painters, produced small biblical works, which are beautiful in form and colour and strike an ideal middle course between sentiment and cold purity as in *Joash drawing the Bow* (Hamburg, Pl. 56A). His style was to change under Pre-Raphaelite influence. The indignant outcry of Charles Dickens against Millais' *Carpenter's Shop* shows how even an intelligent mind could react to a change in accepted fashions. It is not perhaps surprising that the Pre-Raphaelites should have found their main patrons amongst the new rich manufacturers from industrial cities, whose minds were less encumbered by knowledge of earlier styles and fashions in painting.

4. *Literary and Historical*. The eighteenth-century habit of depicting scenes from literature in a markedly theatrical manner, and with the characters wearing clothes reminiscent more of the prop basket than of the period of history portrayed, dissolved into two streams. The influence of Charles Robert Leslie is very

apparent in both trends. One of these was pure illustration born of the painter's imagination and inspired by his readings. Illustrations to novels and plays were increasingly popular during this period and reflect the current trends in domestic reading and family playgoing. Shakespeare was still popular, but the other authors so much favoured by the earlier generation gave way to Cervantes, Molière, Sterne and Addison. The greatest favourites were the ever-popular *Vicar of Wakefield* and, more strangely, *Gil Blas*. Thackeray became so tired of scenes from the last two that he threatened never to notice any of them again. However, his good resolution was shattered when he saw and greatly admired William Mulready's two scenes from Goldsmith in the Academies of 1844 and 1847, *The Whistonian Controversy* and *Burchell and Sophia in the Fields* (which are in the collection of Lord Northbrook), two of his best works, fine in colour and capturing the spirit of the novel. *Choosing the Wedding Gown* (Victoria and Albert Museum, London), a scene from the same book, is an equally charming and affectionate rendering. Leslie's *Autolycus* (1836, Bethnal Green Museum, London), is one of the best of all nineteenth-century attempts to illustrate Shakespeare on a modest scale. The pictures in this stream, although by the very nature of things somewhat dated, have none the less a timeless quality that best serves an author or a reader at the hands of an illustrator.

The next group to be noticed were more theatrical, or perhaps it would be clearer to describe them as charades taking place in the painter's studio. The men and women are clearly models dressed up and have the marked self-conscious air of dancers at a fancy-dress ball. W. P. Frith was a bad offender in this respect, and even the quality of his painting will not efface this conclusion. Towards the end of his long life this feeling of dressing-up became more marked and was the parent of academy period pieces which one associates with children in mob caps and Marcus Stone and E. A. Abbey. E. M. Ward is never at ease in the world of the French Revolution, which he loved to depict, and one can never feel the tragedy of the *Family in the Temple*; but infinitely preferable is his portrait of *Lord Lytton* (Knebworth – Pl. 61B). Augustus Egg, however, in *Queen Elizabeth Discovers that She is no longer Young*, has achieved a more timeless and truly historical illustration.

5. *Academic.* The main exponent of academic historical painting was William Etty. He was born in York in 1787, and was to remain devoted to his native city for the whole of his life. His painting life was built around the life-class of the Royal Academy, where he devoted himself to "God's most glorious work, Woman". A visit to Italy instilled into him a love of Venetian colouring, and his subsequent work was to unite this rich colouring with academic forms. His grand compositions reflected overmuch the conscious posing of his models and, therefore, robbed them of spontaneity. But his appeal was more to the senses than to the intellect. His work is far more romantic than coldly classical and his paint is juicy, glowing and

fluent. His greatest works are his *Judgement of Paris* (Port Sunlight, Cheshire), *Pandora* (Leeds) and *Judith* (Edinburgh); though one of his most memorable canvases is the *Hero and Leander* (Mrs E. J. Britten – Pl. 60B), which is both romantic and dramatic and yet academically posed. His many male and female nude studies, often left unfinished and then tidied up by lesser hands, have flooded the dealers in recent times and caused his reputation to be engulfed. His landscape and still-life painting have been neglected and his portraiture has only recently been re-valued. In a work such as *The Repentant Prodigal's Return to his Father* (Ashmolean Museum, Oxford), which relies on no academic nudes, we can appreciate his gift for straightforward narrative in the simplest terms, and his rich handling of paint. Etty must always remain an isolated figure, and yet in his knowledge and application he remains essentially an artist of his own time.

Genre Painting. The painting of scenes from English everyday life did not really become popular until the early years of the nineteenth century. This new demand was probably inspired by Dutch cabinet pictures of the seventeenth century which were being collected by certain discerning connoisseurs led by the Regent. In 1812, Edward Bird painted *Choristers Rehearsing*, which was bought by the Regent; a companion was commissioned but never finished. Bird, in fact, preferred painting scenes from Shakespeare and from history. The most important English genre artist, David Wilkie, was born in the manse at Cults, Fife, in 1785. His earliest work was influenced by engravings after Teniers and Ostade. *Pitlessie Fair*, painted when he was only nineteen, is an astonishingly able composition, but the colour range shows clearly that he knew Teniers only through the engraver. In London, where he settled in 1804, he quickly established his reputation and found patrons eager to buy or commission his scenes from Scottish peasant life. His treatment was free from the rustic sweetness and "Petit Trianon-like" make-believe of the previous century; but they are filled with anecdote and humour, bordering sometimes on caricature, to make them completely palatable. They were never to startle or dismay in the way that Courbet was to startle Paris when he painted the inhabitants of Ornans. Courbet depicted his peasants in a strictly realistic way, without subsidiary anecdote, and on a scale usually associated with history painting. George IV purchased Wilkie's *Penny Wedding* and *Blind Man's Buff* for the royal collection, and he was the first artist of his generation to be hung in the National Gallery. His early works are tightly painted, and the amount of thought that went into their composition can be gauged from the innumerable pen-and-chalk drawings and oil studies which he did as preliminary workings. Wilkie, in fact, almost equals Rubens in the amount of preparatory work that went towards the finished composition. His style broadened after a visit to Spain and Italy, and still found favour with George IV who purchased several examples. It was held in his lifetime, and by many today, that his style deteriorated.

Thackeray, as he surveyed Wilkie's later work, sighed for the earlier genre and found his looser brush work, muddier colour and Rembrandtesque lighting a sad tumble from the incident-packed earlier canvases. His middle and later works are in fact, very fine, and one of them, *Peep O' Day Boy's Cabin* (1836, Tate Gallery) can make some claims to be his masterpiece. His last rich colourful sketches and drawings were not seen by the public and critics until the posthumous sale of his works a year after his death and burial at sea, in 1841. His wash drawings (Pl. 57A) have deservedly come to be much sought after today.

William Mulready, an Irishman, worked at first in a style directed by Wilkie's earlier phase. He was, in fact, to change his method of painting several times, but always, after some initial stumbling, to master it. He worked on a small scale with no further ambition than to depict a scene with sympathy and clarity. His scenes from contemporary life had no social message and are painted with a glowing sense of colour and with perfect underlying drawing. His soundness as an academic draughtsman gives a greater solidarity to his work and raises him above his imitators. He was not only the perfect illustrator to Goldsmith, but he could render in *The Sonnet* (Victoria and Albert Museum) all the tenderness and embarrassment of young love, as well as the expectation and shyness of reading a self-revelatory poem. He was also fond of depicting the joys and squabbles of children as in *A Dog of Two Minds* (1830, Liverpool). Redgrave found violence and a lack of social consciousness in his work and complained that his peasants were too refined. To some extent this point of view is perhaps true and is indicative of his own uneasy temperament, but his pictures give, today, the same pleasure that they gave to his contemporaries. Apart from his anecdotal work, his *Interior of an English Cottage*, purchased by George IV, remains one of his most hauntingly lovely pictures, with its still serenity and soft pink light.

Thomas Webster was another faithful recorder of village life, and his *Village Choir* (Victoria and Albert Museum) and *The Playground* (Christopher Loyd) continue to remain popular favourites. B. R. Haydon in *Punch* and *Chairing the Member* moved from the grand style into London Life. Edwin Landseer painted shepherds in their natural surroundings in the Highlands as well as royal sporting occasions. His animals often hovered on the wrong side of sentimentality, but were lovingly and beautifully rendered. Richard Redgrave was far more direct in his appeal to sentiment, finding his heroines amongst mournful widows and depressed governesses. Augustus Leopold Egg became the friend and patron of the early Pre-Raphaelites, and his own style altered under their impact. In his new style he painted *The Travelling Companions* (Birmingham), two young ladies in their carriage passing the Mentone coast oblivious of the scenery, and his dramatic *Past and Present* (Tate), a commentary in three canvases on the sadness of children when their parents fail to keep sacred the marriage vow. R. B. Martineau also pursued a similar subject in *The Last Day in the Old Home* (Tate), but his more pleasing works are *Picciola* (Tate, Pl. 57B) and *Kit's Writing Lesson* (Tate). The sincerity and skill of these works were almost buried by the social documentaries and moralizing sermons exhibited by many of their brother artists in the annual Academy.

William Collins, the father of Wilkie and Charles Alston, is of an earlier generation, but his peaceful scenes of country and seashore are a happy blend of genre and landscape and are some of the more pleasant and unassuming works of their time.

One artist has enjoyed an almost continual popularity for his scenes from Victorian life. W. P. Frith left in his *Autobiography* a vivid account of his work from the early days and fame to the end of his long life when he had somewhat outlived the esteem of the critics. *Ramsgate Sands* (Buckingham Palace); *Derby Day* (Tate); and *The Railway Station* (Royal Holloway College, London) are always assured of an affectionate place in any anthology of Victorian painting. Nor must this sentiment for his work make one blind to his ability to compose and paint.

The Pre-Raphaelite painters and Ford Madox Brown were all fascinated by scenes from contemporary life. Rossetti dragged himself from his studies of the Arthurian legends and of Dante to work on the moral picture *Found* (Bancroft Foundation, Wilmington, Delaware, U.S.A.), which was partly based on a poem by William Bell Scott. Holman Hunt went even farther in preaching his moral in *The Awakening Conscience* (Sir Colin Anderson, London); but the great masterpiece in this vein to be produced by any member of the brotherhood is *The Blind Girl* (City Art Gallery, Birmingham) by J. E. Millais, a touching and yet unsentimental rendering of two tired figures seated in a landscape bathed in the light of a rainbow.

The Pre-Raphaelites. The term Pre-Raphaelite has been used, for far too long, as a convenient label attached to an untidy parcel of artists, flourishing between 1848 and 1880, many of whom had, in fact, nothing in common and whose painting sprang from different roots. The appellation Pre-Raphaelite should, in fact, belong only to the original Brotherhood, and not to Morris and Burne-Jones and their followers. The Brotherhood was formed in 1848 and consisted of W. Holman Hunt, J. E. Millais, D. G. Rossetti, Thomas Woolner, F. G. Stephens, James Collinson and W. M. Rossetti. In 1850 their literary organ *The Germ* ceased to be produced and the Brotherhood was fast dissolving; by 1852 it was extinct. "So now," as D. G. Rossetti wrote, "the whole Round Table was dissolved." The limited aims of these seven men have been stretched far farther than the facts warrant, and the secret letters P.R.B., which occur on only three of their paintings, once revealed, have been taken into the bosom of art history and used in a way that would have amazed them in later life; all of them, with the exception of Hunt, considered it only a boyish enthusiasm. The original members of 1848 looked with disfavour at the annual exhibitions of the Royal Academy and in fact at all the damage that had been done to art since the time of Raphael. They floundered into a vague idea of early Christian art which was crystallized when they found a book of indifferent engravings by Lasinio, after the mural paintings in the Campo Santo at Pisa. These were Pre-Raphael, and so the name was born.

J. E. Millais was almost an infant prodigy. At sixteen he painted *Pizarro Seizing the Inca of Peru*, a remarkable performance perhaps influenced by Henry Perronet Briggs' *First Conference between the Spaniards and Peruvians*, 1826 (Pl. 56B). His early paintings and his masterly angular drawings are truly "Pre-Raphael" (Pl. 48A) in spirit and touched with the lyrical beauty of Keats and Tennyson, his favourite poets, and their names conjure up the glowing jewel-like medieval world of his imagination – *Lorenzo and Isabella*; *Mariana*; *Ophelia*; and *The Return of the Dove to the Ark*. The furore caused by *The Carpenter's Shop* died down and was followed by his election to the Royal Academy in 1853. His marriage to Mrs Ruskin, and perhaps the new-found cares of family life, caused him to follow the amazing fluency of his brush and to become an over prolific painter of subject pieces and portraits. Sadder still was the extinction of his earlier gifts of poetry and imagination, which gave way, after 1857, to some unforgivable sentiment, when the voice of Keats was muffled by Tupper. Not all his later painting is bad; his technical ability never left him. He is reported to have said to Lady Constance Leslie, as he left, in tears, the retrospective exhibition of his work in 1886, "In looking at my earliest pictures I have been overcome with chagrin that I so far failed in my maturity to fulfil the forecast of my youth."

William Holman Hunt pursued to the end of his life what he believed to be the original aims of the Brotherhood. Like Millais, he studied nature closely, accepting and depicting everything seen, selecting or rejecting nothing, and firmly believing in the hard toil of obtaining verisimilitude of fact. His early work is ambitious and his composition and grouping in *Rienzi* and *The Converted British Family* is remarkably effective. His imagination was on a higher level than any other member of the Brotherhood, but his work was overladen by the very painstaking method he chose to adopt, and the lyrical moments which he achieved in *The Hireling Shepherd* were soon swamped by his exact reportage from the Holy Land. He saw colour "without eyelids", and the resulting harshness detracts from his merit as a painter. In addition, the woollen garments worn by his figures have the quality and appearance of having been knitted from wire mesh and detract from his ability to paint the human face.

Dante Gabriel Rossetti was both painter and poet, and his enthusiasm soon overcame his early stumblings. To both Hunt and Millais, overawed by his infectious but suspicious temperament, he must have seemed only an amateur. He was deeply read in Dante and the Arthurian legends; and in the beauty of his future wife, Elizabeth Siddal, he found his ideal Beatrice and Guenevere. The glowing

H

colours of his water colours found many admirers, including Ruskin, though the latter failed to mould the character of his protegé in the way he would have liked. *Dante Drawing an Angel*, *Leah and Rachel* and *Sir Galahad* are amongst the finest of these works, far surpassing the *Girlhood of the Virgin Mary* or *Ecce Ancilla Domini*, which were his first major works before he met Miss Siddal. The many studies of his wife are amongst his best drawings; "Drawers and drawers of lovely Guggums", as Madox Brown observed. The long illness of Elizabeth Siddal, which ended in her death in 1862, witnessed a change in Rossetti's style, and the face and dark hair of Jane Morris came to dominate his work. His later style was coarser, and the early medieval vision was buried under the large-scale portraits of his favourite models, who were labelled with exotic-sounding names.

Of the rest of the Pre-Raphaelite Brotherhood little need be said; Collinson and Stephens painted only a few pictures; Woolner was a sculptor and W. M. Rossetti never painted, but was to be the faithful friend and chronicler of the whole movement.

Two other painters were on the fringe of the movement, Walter Deverell who died young, and Arthur Hughes. Hughes was one of the most delightful artists, and his early work is full of a poetic beauty which was to leave him towards the close of his long life. His early lyrical works are never too obvious in sentiment or lacking in craftsmanship. How nearly he bordered disaster is apparent in his titles, *Home from Sea*, *The Tryst*, and *April Love*; but his triumphant handling of his subject matter gives him an assured place in the group.

Ford Madox Brown was never a Pre-Raphaelite, though he was often classed as one. His training had been in Belgium, and his work reflects the current continental theories closely: his *Chaucer* is a very German picture. Much emphasis has been laid on the influence of German painters, such as Cornelius and Overbeck, on the Brotherhood, but their aims, apart from a sort of cousinly resemblance, are not really apparent except in Brown. Brown was the lifelong friend of Rossetti, but to the end of his days he refrained from identifying himself with any section of the art world. His greatest contribution lies perhaps in his landscape painting (see page 116), which is redolent of his great clarity of vision, though sometimes marred by violent use of colour. His scenes from everyday life and from history are well drawn and composed, but rather spoiled by the toothy grimaces of his figures. Brown's influence was negligible, but, none the less, he remains the most considerable figure of the period.

The sight of Millais' *Return of the Dove to the Ark* in an Oxford shop caused two Oxford undergraduates, Edward Burne-Jones and William Morris, to devote the rest of their lives to art. Burne-Jones was influenced in his early work by Rossetti, whom he admired as an artist and loved as a man, but his roots were entirely different from the Pre-Raphaelites and sprang from his visit to Italy and his admiration for Botticelli and Mantegna. His pale, elongated and wide-eyed beauties have often, mistakenly, been held up as the ideal Pre-Raphaelite type. Subtle as a draughtsman, it was his misfortune to drive his talents towards compositions which were far too large in scale to house his imagination comfortably. His subject-matter was set in a timeless age and he was content, unlike the Brotherhood, to tell a story as a story-book picture and not as a projection of probability. His attainments lie outside the period and his influence was to continue for many years.

Landscape. The landscapes shown each year at the Royal Academy were dominated by those of the veteran J. M. W. Turner until he ceased to exhibit in 1850. His later works clearly demonstrate, year by year, his attempts to render light at the expense of form. Such famous works as *The Fighting Téméraire, Rain, Steam and Speed*, and the *Interiors at Petworth* were done at this time. John Constable died suddenly in 1837, and the rising generation could not be thought the equal of two such undoubted masters. However, the early Victorians demanded landscapes, with or without figures and animals, which had a straightforward rendering of nature and the elements and the simple rustic life for the adornment of their rooms. The atmospheric effects of Constable or the frenzy of light in a Turner were not nearly so comprehensible as the mediocre landscapes of Augustus Callcott. Callcott was knighted in 1837, and it is not at all easy now to understand his popularity or reputation. His wife, Maria Graham, better known as the author of *Little Arthur's History of England*, was an important influence on young artists, whom she asked to her home and whose careers she encouraged. Thomas Creswick and F. R. Lee were other popular but commonplace artists. So many painters added to the vast output of landscape painting during these thirty years that it is impossible to chronicle their work. Reference must, however, be made to the Romantic vision of Francis Danby as well as to his depiction of the sea in both its gentle calm and its rock-grazing fierceness. His *Upas Tree* (Victoria and Albert Museum) is a sad wreck but *Disappointed Love* in the same collection will serve as an example of his vein of romantic sensibility. In *The Sixth Seal* (Dublin) he essayed a John Martin-like biblical explosion, the full effect of which is now obscured by grime. E. W. Cooke painted the calm of a shore liberally strewn with lobster-pots, and T. Sidney Cooper was to spend the ninety-nine years of his life recording the placid existence of cows in the English landscape. Cooper's "cowscapes", as they are so often termed, have been too easily despised. He is vastly superior to the hoard of Highland-cattle painters who arose to decorate the English dining-room. Painters not always associated with landscape also made considerable contributions. Landseer, the painter of domestic and wild animals, produced some exquisite landscapes; and Eastlake varied his rather bookish historical style with views of the monuments of his much-loved Rome. Richard Redgrave also occasionally left his over-sentimentalized interior scenes to paint the landscape outside. This he did feelingly, as in *Valleys Thick with Corn* (Birmingham), though his hand lacked the necessary breadth of touch.

Certain painters travelled extensively abroad. James Holland found his inspiration by the canals of Venice, where he painted with a richly loaded palette, making an interesting comparison with the effervescent effects of Turner. W. J. Muller varied his style between passable attempts in the manner of Constable and reportage of life in the Near East. A composition with a Bedouin encampment, an oasis and a palm-tree was almost certain of an immediate sale.

The Romantic artists of the previous twenty years outlived the poetry of their early work. John Linnell lived until 1882, and his work became less spontaneous, but seldom dull. His son-in-law, Samuel Palmer, died a year earlier and, although he is rightly most esteemed for the work he did under deep inspiration and religious intensity of feeling at Shoreham in the 'twenties and 'thirties, his later work in both Italy and England shows a grasp of medium which should not be undervalued. His water colours done in Rome are especially skilful and mirror the feelings of English artists for the monuments and people of the eternal city, the mecca of so many artists. His illustrations to Milton are over-hot in colour, with a preponderance of purple, and far the least pleasing of his work.

The importance of landscape in the work of the Pre-Raphaelites is discussed under that heading, but it can be stressed that Madox Brown is probably the best landscape painter of the period, even if the intensity of his colour is at first inspection rather too rich and raw. *Walton-on-the-Naze* (Birmingham), *The Hayfield* (S. J. Gillum, Esq.), above all *An English Autumn Afternoon* (Birmingham), are remarkable achievements. They show all the necessary "truth to nature", and because there is no breaking down into irritating and scientific detail they preserve the largeness of a sympathetic and loving vision. John Brett is the exact opposite, following slavishly the teachings of Ruskin and demonstrating a painstaking understanding of the underlying geology. William Dyce in *Pegwell Bay* (Tate) also shows an acute feeling for landscape but with a shade too much precision of touch at the expense of atmospheric effect. Madox Brown called his own *English Afternoon* "a literal transcript of the scenery round London, as looked at from Hampstead. The smoke is seen rising halfway above the fantastic shaped, small distant cumuli, which accompany particularly fine weather. The upper portion of the sky would be blue, as seen reflected in the youth's hat, the grey mist of Autumn only rising a certain height. The time is 3 p.m., when late in October the shadows already lie long, and the sun's rays (coming from behind us in this work) are preternaturally glowing, as in rivalry of the foliage. The figures are peculiarly English – they are hardly lovers – mere boy and girl neighbours and friends."

Travellers abroad. During the first thirty years of the nineteenth century many English artists made the pilgrimage to Rome, and several stayed there for long periods. They painted scenes from peasant life, sketched in the Campagna, and searched for models on the Spanish Steps. Several published letters and memoirs testify to their life there. Eastlake, indeed, seems to have been inspired to paint *The Spartan Isadas* (Chatsworth) after a rather similar incident had happened in a fire at Joseph Severn's house, but his best works are taken from the life around him. *Pilgrims in First Sight of Rome* (Woburn Abbey) and *Peasant Woman Fainting from the Bite of a Snake* (Victoria and Albert Museum) are two of his most attractive canvases, which mirror the life he and his fellow artists sought and which inspired their subject-matter. Thomas Unwins is now a neglected and forgotten artist, but his *A Neapolitan Boy Decorating the Head of his Inamorata* and *An Italian Mother Teaching her Child the Tarantella*, both in the Victoria and Albert Museum, testify to his gaiety and sense of colour. Severn, forgetting Keats for a moment, produced a hauntingly romantic *Shelley in Rome* (Keats–Shelley House, Rome). The inspiration they found in Rome was to be taken up by American artists, who also gathered there and formed a similar colony. Later in the century Spain and the Near East were to draw John Frederick Lewis. Wilkie records in his letters his meeting with this artist, who had been absent from England so long. His works glow with a richer colour than those of any other artist, and today tend to be difficult to hang in other company for that reason. In fact, he achieved and recorded much more than Holman Hunt on the same territory. *The Doubtful Coin* (Birmingham) and *The Siesta* (Tate) are two excellent examples of his virtuosity. John Phillip, a Scotsman, spent most of his days in Spain, but his work is more *mouvmente* and fussy in grouping. His scenes are studied from a picturesque angle of the ceremonies he witnessed, whilst Lewis preferred anecdotal reportage.

SCULPTURE

JOHN WOODWARD

FOUR sculptors were to continue their craftsmanship into the period 1830–60, which, in fact, saw some of their finest works. Sir Francis Chantrey died in 1841 and his masterpiece *Mrs Jordan* (Earl of Munster) was completed ten years earlier, and his delicate bust of *Robert Southey* (National Portrait Gallery, London) dates from 1831. William Behnes lived until 1864, his busts and statues sometimes showing the delicacy of his earlier years, but at others demonstrating the dangers of over-productivity in a rather insensitive lumpiness. His bust of *Prince George of Cumberland* (Windsor, Pl. 63A) shows his skill with children. Samuel Joseph's two finest statues date from 1833 and 1842 respectively, namely his *William Wilberforce* (Westminster Abbey) and *David Wilkie* (Tate). A recent acquisition by the Victoria and Albert Museum is his bust of *George IV* (1831), a swagger piece which is almost a Lawrence done over in marble. John Gibson continued to be the doyen of English artists in Rome until 1866. His American pupil Harriet Hosmer described him as "A God in his Studio but Heaven help him out of it". His inability to cope with everyday life caused a railway porter in Italy to inquire if he was a foreigner. "No," replied Gibson, "I am not a foreigner, I am a sculptor." Twice he returned to England to make statues of Queen Victoria (Pl. 62B), the earlier of which he "tinted" in the same way as his *Venus*. His great *Hunter and his Dog* dates from 1843.

The new generation produced no men as remarkable as these, though there was a continual demand for memorials, statues, busts and decorative works. The plethora of commissions seems almost to have deadened ingenuity, and the weight of white marble left in the churches and houses of England was to cause the best work to be unjustly neglected in a too-sweeping condemnation of the bulk.

E. H. Bailey was both a decorative and monumental sculptor. His work is uneven, but at its best comes close in quality to Chantrey. He made the statue of Nelson in Trafalgar Square. An excellent example of his wall monuments is that to the Earl of Pomfret (1830, Easton Neston). Joseph Durham trained under Bailey, and executed some worthy work, the best known being his statue of the Prince Consort in front of the Albert Hall. *Waiting his Innings* (City of London School, Pl. 64C) is a charming rendering of youth, free of the sentiment that was soon to overwhelm nearly all sculpture of children, and his accuracy of detail ensures that even the studs in the boots are carefully sculpted. Resurrected for exhibition in Holland Park in 1957, it showed a surprising solidarity and perfection. On the other side of the Albert Hall towers the Albert Memorial, and John Foley was responsible for the statue of the Prince Consort, which was finished after his death, and which falls below his statue of Charles Barry in the Houses of Parliament. Much of his work is of the historical fancy-dress variety and fails to be convincing. A posthumous statue looks far more of an artificial fabrication than most painted historical scenes, and it would be a great boon to the world if worthy Societies would not attempt to commemorate the famous but long-dead by commissioning posthumous monuments and persuading deans to erect them. It may make good the neglect of an earlier age, but is seldom an ornament or a pleasure. The decoration of the new Houses of Parliament with statues of famous fighters for liberty, for two of which Foley is responsible, was a dismal error. His statues of Outram and Hardinge are in Calcutta. Patrick Macdowell is best known for his *Flora* in the Royal Academy, and although his brother artist, Henry Weekes, considered that he "makes his appeal to our best and noblest feelings", this claim appears to be excessive. Weekes himself produced one of the best memorial busts of the period, *Robert Southey* (Westminster Abbey).

William Theed the younger was another pupil of Bailey, but he increased his knowledge of the neo-classical school by studying under Thorwalsden and Gibson.

The influence of this school can be seen in his *Narcissus* (Buckingham Palace, Pl. 64A). He later left the neo-classical school and his *Queen Victoria and Prince Albert* in Anglo-Saxon costume, now in the Frogmore Mausoleum, Windsor, is one of his most startling works in a new manner. Richard Wyatt also studied in Rome, under Canova and Thorwalsden, and, like Gibson, settled there. He achieved fame late, but his *Glysera* and *Penelope* were both purchased by the Queen. Of the latter, the Hon. Georgiana Lidell wrote: "Such a beautiful statue arrived here yesterday from Rome, a full length statue of Penelope by Wyatt, standing in a pensive attitude,

An illustration by Arthur Hughes from *Enoch Arden* by Alfred Tennyson.
Published by Edward Moxon, London, 1866.

with one hand on her heart and the other holding a crook, with a fine dog looking up in her face, the drapery is exceedingly graceful, and the expression of her beautiful countenance very lovely but sad. The Queen is much pleased with it and it is considered Wyatt's *chef d'œuvre*."

John Lough was a controversial figure in his lifetime, either praised or execrated to excess by sections of the Press. His work could certainly be ludicrous and fussily flamboyant at times. *Milo* (Blagdon) is a fine work of great power, now shown magnificently in a setting by Lutyens, and his finest monument is that to Bishop Middleton (St Paul's Cathedral, London), the first Protestant Bishop of India, blessing two members of his great diocese. This, although somewhat cumbersome, has strength and proves the sculptural possibilities of lawn sleeves. John Edward Carew was befriended by the Earl of Egremont up to the latter's death in 1837. Unfortunately, he made a consummate fool of himself in trying to extract money from the Earl's executors. He was a sculptor of originality and charm as can be seen by his *Adonis and the Boar* (1826, Petworth, Sussex, Pl. 64B) and the bust of Henry Wyndham (1831, Petworth, Pl. 62A).

The tastes for neo-classic and Renaissance ran side by side and never really resolved itself during this period. Royal taste turned towards Baron Marochetti and Jacob Boehme, worthy but pedestrian men. The one talent to span the time between the older generation and the appearance of Alfred Stevens was that of Thomas Woolner, an original member of the Pre-Raphaelite Brotherhood. In 1852 he set sail to make his fortune in the Australian gold-fields. When this failed to be the lucrative adventure he had supposed, he returned to England and sculpture. His work rightly still enjoys a considerable reputation, and his busts, on their characteristic socles, are always rewarding to study. *Tennyson* (Trinity College, Cambridge, Pl. 63B); *Newman* (Keble College, Oxford); and *Gladstone* on his splendid pedestal ornamented with bas-reliefs from the *Iliad* (Ashmolean) are perhaps his deepest character studies. His monuments are less pleasing. The minor Pre-Raphaelite sculptor Alexander Munro made the charming fountain in Berkeley Square, and amongst his other work is the bust of his wife (Mrs Munro, Oxford), which has a fresh spontaneity rare at this time. Recently his group *Paolo and Francesca* (1851) has come to light and is the most Pre-Raphaelite piece of sculpture known. Paolo's face registers a suitable anguish.

For Further Reading

PAINTING

Painting in Britain 1530–1790 by Ellis Waterhouse, Penguin Books, London, 1953.

English Art 1625–1714 by Margaret Whinney and Oliver Millar, Oxford University Press, 1957.

Aspects of Art in England c. 1700–1850, B.B.C., London, 1950.

Tudor Artists by E. Auerbach, Athlone Press of the University of London, 1954.

English Taste in Landscape in the Seventeenth Century by Henry V. S. and Margaret S. Ogden, Oxford University Press, 1955.

Early Conversation Pieces by Ralph Edwards, Country Life, London, 1954.

Animal Painting in England by Basil Taylor, Penguin Books, London, 1955.

Early English Watercolours by J. O. Williams, The Connoisseur, London, 1952.

Pre-Raphaelite Painting by R. Ironside and J. Gere, Phaidon Press, London, 1948.

Painters of the Victorian Scene by G. Reynolds, Batsford, London, 1953.

SCULPTURE

English Art 1625–1714 by Margaret Whinney and Oliver Millar, Oxford University Press, 1957.

Dictionary of British Sculptors 1660–1851 by R. Gunnis, Odhams Press, London, 1953.

English Monumental Sculpture since the Renaissance by K. A. Esdaile, S.P.C.K., London, 1927.

The Life and Works of Louis François Roubiliac by K. A. Esdaile, Oxford University Press, 1928.

Michael Rysbrack by M. I. Webb, Country Life, London, 1954.

Acknowledgements

The Editor and the Publishers of this volume thank the individuals and other owners listed below for kindly allowing them to use the plates specified:

Thomas Agnew and Sons Ltd for plate 18; His Grace the Lord Archbishop of Canterbury for plate 6B; The Ashmolean Museum, Oxford, for plate 48; Bodleian Library, Oxford, for plate 7A; the British Museum for plate 3B; Lt-Col. Sir Walter Bromley-Davenport for plate 16A; Christ Church, Oxford, for plate 35A; City Art Gallery, Bristol, for plate 4; City of Leicester Art Gallery for plate 33; City of London School for plate 64; City of York Art Gallery for plate 51A; Sir Kenneth Clark for plate 59; The Controller of H.M. Stationery Office for plates 9, 11, 20 and 24A, from The Royal Commission on Historical Monuments' Inventory of Historical Monuments in Dorset, Essex and (the last two plates) Middlesex respectively; Corporation of Liverpool for plate 61B; Courtauld Institute of Art for plates 8, 24B and 32; The Governors of the Thomas Coram Foundation for Children for plate 31; The House of Lords for plate 54B; Sir Gyles Isham for plate 35B; Kunsthalle, Hamburg, for plate 56A; Leeds City Art Gallery for plates 34A, 38B, 40A and 41A; R. Leon Esq. for plate 15B; The Marquess of Bath for plate 15A; The Earl of Mexborough for plate 39A; The Ministry of Works for plate 7B (Crown copyright reserved); The Earl of Munster for plate 50; the Museum and Art Gallery, Birmingham, for plate 57A; National Art Gallery, Sydney, for plate 27A; National Buildings Record for plates 10 and 21B; The Trustees, The National Gallery, for plates 47A and 47B; National Gallery of Scotland for plates 46, 47C and 55A; National Maritime Museum for plate 29; National Museum of Wales for plates 28A and 36A; National Portrait Gallery for plates 1A, 1B, 3C, 26A, 45B and 60A; The National Trust for plate 14B; National Trust and A. C. Cooper for plate 22A; The Duke of Northampton for plates 13A and 14A; North Carolina Museum of Art for plate 17; The Duke of Northumberland for plate 13B; Rev. H. V. P. Nunn for plate 21A; The Hon. Clive Pearson, Parham, for plate 12; the Petworth Collection for plates 61A and 62B; Radio Times Hulton Picture Library for plate 41B; Prado, Madrid, for plate 3A; Photo Precision Ltd for plate 25A; President and Council of the Royal Academy for plate 43C; The Provost and Fellows of Eton College for plate 37; Her Majesty the Queen for plates 2A, 6A, 34B, 39B, 43A, 54A, 62A and 63A; J. C. Quilter Esq. for plate 51B; The Earl of Radnor for plate 2C; Messrs Rosenberg and Stiebel Inc., New York, for plate 45A; Royal Society of Arts for plate 40B; Syndics of the Fitzwilliam Museum, Cambridge, for plate 22B; Temple Newsam House, Leeds, for plate 38A; Sir Anthony Tichborne for plate 19B; Trinity College, Cambridge, for plate 63B; the Trustees of the Chatsworth Settlement for plates 16B, 28B, 30A and 44B; the Trustees of the Tate Gallery for plates 26B, 36B, 53, 56B, 57B, 58A, 58B and 60B; Dr Pamela Tudor-Craig for plate 23; University of Glasgow for plate 43B; Urban District Council of Rickmansworth for plate 30B; Viscount de L'Isle for plate 49; Wellington Museum for plate 52; The Earl of Warwick for plates 46B and 46C; Executors of the Second Duke of Westminster for plate 44A; The Worshipful Company of Painter-Stainers for plate 25B; The Earl of Yarborough for plate 2B; Musées Royaux des Beaux-Arts, Brussels for plate 19; Lady Hermione Cobbold for Plate 61B; Mrs. E. J. Britten for plate 60B.

The Publishers regret that in a few instances their efforts to contact the present owners of objects shown in the plates for permission to include them in this series have not been successful. However, due acknowledgment will be made in any future editions if they are notified.

Index

THE PLATES

PLATE IA. HANS HOLBEIN, 1537. Henry VIII and
Henry VII (cartoon for the Whitehall wall-painting).

PLATE IB. Artist unknown, c. 1530–35.
Margaret Pole, Countess of Salisbury.

I

PLATE 2B. HE, 1549. A Turk on horseback.

PLATE 2A. HANS HOLBEIN, c. 1538–40.
George Brooke, Lord Cobham.

PLATE 2C. HE, 1550. Thomas Wyndham.

PLATE 3A. ANTONIO MOR, 1554. Queen Mary I.

PLATE 3B. FEDERICO ZUCCARO,
c. 1574. Queen Elizabeth I.

PLATE 3C. GERLACH FLICKE, c. 1547.
Archbishop Cranmer.

PLATE 4A. Artist unknown, *c.* 1570. A morality.

PLATE 4B. ANTONIO DA SOLARIO, 1514. The Withypol triptych.

PLATE 5A. HE, 1562. Margaret, Duchess of Norfolk.

PLATE 5B. Artist unknown, c. 1547. Henry VIII on his death-bed, Edward VI and his council, and the Pope.

PLATE 6A. GUILLIM SCROTS or STRETES, *c.* 1550.
Edward VI.

PLATE 6B. HANS HOLBEIN, 1527.
Archbishop Warham.

PLATE 7A. CORNELIUS KETEL, 1577.
Sir Martin Frobisher.

PLATE 7B. GEORGE GOWER, c. 1577.
Sir Thomas Cornwallis.

PLATE 8. Tomb of the Earl of Rutland, Bottesford, Leicestershire, by Richard Parker.

PLATE 9. Tomb of Sir John Jefferey,
Whitchurch Canonicorum, Dorset,
c. 1611.

HERE LYETH THE BODY
OF S. IOHN IEFFEREY OF
CATHERSTONE KNIGHT
WHO DYED THE 7 OF
MAY, AN DNI 161C

PLATE 10. Daughters of Lord Teynham on his tomb at Lynsted, Kent, by Epiphanius Evesham.

PLATE 11. Tomb of Lord Marney, Layer Marney,
Essex. Early sixteenth century.

PLATE 12. DANIEL MYTENS. Charles I (1623?).
(Canvas 71 in. × 56 in.)

PLATE 13A. CORNELIUS JOHNSON. Spencer, 2nd Earl of Northampton (1633). (Canvas 30¾ in. × 25½ in.)

PLATE 13B. SIR PETER LELY. James, Duke of York (1647). (Canvas 28¼ in. × 23¾ in.)

PLATE 14A. SIR PETER LELY. Robert, 2nd Earl of Sunderland. (Canvas 48½ in. × 39¼ in.)

PLATE 14B. WILLIAM DOBSON. James, 3rd Earl of Northampton. (Canvas 45½ in. × 36¼ in.)

PLATE 15A. JOHN RILEY. Sir William Coventry. (Canvas 50 in. × 40 in.)

PLATE 15B. GERARD SOEST. John Bulwer. (Canvas 50 in. × 40 in.)

PLATE 16A. JONATHAN RICHARDSON. The artist and his son in the presence of
Milton. (Canvas 25 in. × 30 in.)

PLATE 16B. LOUIS LAGUERRE. The State Bedroom.

PLATE 17. SIR ANTHONY VAN DYCK. Mary, Duchess of Richmond, with Lord Arran.
(Canvas 83 in. × 40 in.)

K

PLATE 18A. JAN WYCK. The stag hunt. (Canvas $42\frac{1}{2}$ in. $\times$ $67\frac{1}{2}$ in.)

PLATE 18B. GILLIS VAN TILBORCH. The Tichborne Dole (1670). (Canvas 46 in. $\times$ $81\frac{1}{2}$ in.)

PLATE 19. JAN SIBERECHTS. Huntsmen near Longleat (1684). (Canvas 86 in. × 51 in.)

PLATE 20. WILLIAM CURE. Tomb of Sir Roger Aston, died 1612, at Cranford, Middlesex. Southwark work, rich in colour, but coarse in handling.

PLATE 21A. GRINLING GIBBONS. Tomb of Viscount Campden, 1686, at Exton, Rutland. Figures in classical dress.

PLATE 21B. CAIUS GABRIEL CIBBER. The Sackville tomb, 1677, at Withyham, Sussex. A baroque transformation of a traditional type.

PLATE 22A. HUBERT LE SUEUR. Charles I, at Stourhead, Wilts. Smooth and empty in modelling.

PLATE 22B. JOHN BUSHNELL. Charles II. Terracotta, baroque in design and handling.

PLATE 23. HUBERT LE SUEUR. William, 3rd Earl of Pembroke, *c.* 1629, Schools Quadrangle, Oxford. Continental influence in the use of bronze.

PLATE 24A. NICHOLAS STONE. Tomb of Thomas, Lord Knyvett, 1623, at Stanwell, Middlesex. More refined in detail and cutting.

PLATE 24B. JOHN BUSHNELL. Tomb of Lord Mordaunt, died 1675, at Fulham Parish Church, London. A lively baroque design.

PLATE 25A. MAXIMILIAN COLT. Tomb
of Robert Cecil, 1st Earl of Salisbury,
1612, at Hatfield, Herts. A foreign type
in black and white marble. PLATE 25B.
EDWARD PIERCE. Thomas Evans, 1688.
Vigorous in pose and modelling.

PLATE 26A. JOSEPH HIGHMORE.
Samuel Richardson (1750).

PLATE 26B. Attributed to JOSEPH HIGHMORE. Mr Oldham and his friends
(c. 1745).

PLATE 27A. THOMAS HUDSON.
Lady Oxenden (*c.* 1750).

PLATE 27B. WILLIAM HOGARTH. The Levée, the fourth scene from the *Marriage à la Mode* series (1743–5).

PLATE 28A. RICHARD WILSON. Rome and the Ponte Molle (1754).

PLATE 28B. GEORGE LAMBERT (with figures by another hand). Lord Burlington's villa at Chiswick (1742).

PLATE 29. SAMUEL SCOTT. The burning of Payta (1741).

PLATE 30A. GEORGE KNAPTON. The
3rd Earl of Burlington (1743).

PLATE 30B. JACOPO AMIGONI. Jupiter
and Io (1732).

PLATE 31. WILLIAM HOGARTH. Captain Coram (1740).

PLATE 32. MICHAEL RYSBRACK. The model for his Hercules (1744) at
Stourhead.

PLATE 33. L. F. ROUBILIAC. The figure of Religion (1761).

PLATE 34A. L. F. ROUBILIAC.
Alexander Pope (1738).

PLATE 34B. L. F. ROUBILIAC.
Handel (1739).

PLATE 35A. MICHAEL RYSBRACK.
George I (*c.* 1727).

PLATE 35B. PETER SCHEEMAKERS.
Sir Justinian Isham (1737).

PLATE 36A. RICHARD WILSON. Pembroke town and castle (1774).

PLATE 36B. GEORGE STUBBS. Landscape with a gentleman holding his horse (c. 1770).

PLATE 37. GEORGE ROMNEY. Charles Grey, afterwards 2nd Earl Grey (1784).

PLATE 38A. SIR JOSHUA REYNOLDS.
The Marchioness of Hertford (1781).
A portrait which displays the taste for
the noble and grand.

PLATE 38B. J. R. COZENS. Ariccia
(c. 1790), a water-colour landscape.

PLATE 39A. FRANCIS COTES. Lady Stan-
hope and Lady Effingham as Diana and
an attendant (*c.* 1765–70).

PLATE 39B. J. S. COPLEY. The three
princesses (1785).

PLATE 40A. THOMAS GIRTIN. Ripon Minster (1800), a water-colour landscape.

PLATE 40B. JAMES BARRY. The foundation of the Royal Society of Arts (1777–83).

PLATE 41A. FRANCIS TOWNE. The Vale of St John (1786),
a water-colour landscape.

PLATE 41B. The engraving by WILLIAM WOOLLETT (1776) of *The Death of Wolfe*,
painted in 1771 by Benjamin West.

PLATE 42A. JOSEPH NOLLEKENS' Castor and Pollux
(1767) (*Victoria and Albert Museum*), which is based on
a Roman group.

PLATE 42B. JOHN DEARE. Marble relief. Edward and Eleanor (1788).

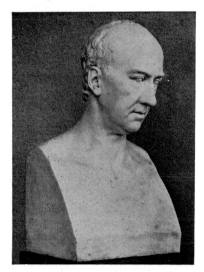

PLATE 43A. JOHN BACON.
George III (1775).

PLATE 43B. CHRISTOPHER HEWETSON.
Gavin Hamilton (1784).

PLATE 43C. THOMAS BANKS. The Falling Titan (1786).

PLATE 44A. RICHARD WESTALL.
Lord Byron.
(Canvas $29\frac{1}{2}$ in. × $24\frac{1}{2}$ in.)

PLATE 44B. C. R. LESLIE. The Grosvenor family.
(Canvas 46 in. × 64 in.)

PLATE 45A. THOMAS PHILLIPS, R.A.
Lady Caroline Lamb.
(Canvas 36 in. × 27½ in.)

PLATE 45B. JOHN SCARLETT DAVIS. The interior of the British Institution Gallery.
(Canvas 43¾ in. × 55 in.)

PLATE 46. JOHN CROME. Castle Eden Dean.
(Water colour on buff paper, 16⅝ in. × 14¾ in.)

PLATE 47A.
JOHN CONSTABLE, R.A.
Malvern Hall, Warwickshire,
from the garden side.
(Canvas 20¼ in. × 30 in.)

PLATE 47B.
JOHN CROME.
Moonrise on the Yare.
(Canvas 28 in. × 43¾ in.)

PLATE 47C.
J. M. W. TURNER.
Somer Hill, Tonbridge.
(Canvas 25 in. × 47 in.)

PLATE 48. WILLIAM BEHNES. Samuel Wooodburn.

PLATE 49. SAMUEL JOSEPH. Lady de L'Isle and Dudley.
Marble, ht 31 in.

PLATE 50. SIR FRANCIS LEGATT CHANTREY, R.A. Mrs Jordan and her family.
Marble, ht 72 in.

PLATE 51A. WILLIAM ETTY.
James Atkinson, 1832.

PLATE 51B. SIR GEORGE HAYTER.
Princess Augusta, 1837.

PLATE 52. SIR DAVID WILKIE. King William IV, 1833.

PLATE 53. G. F. WATTS. Augusta, Lady Castleton, 1846.

PLATE 54A. SIR EDWIN LANDSEER. Van Ambrugh and his animals, 1839.

PLATE 54B. DANIEL MACLISE. Death of Nelson (detail), 1865.

PLATE 55A. DAVID SCOTT. Philoctetes left by the Greek fleet, 1840. PLATE 55B. EDWARD ARMITAGE. Samson "But the Philistine took him", 1851.

A

B

A

PLATE 56A.
WILLIAM   DYCE.
King Joash shoot-
ing the Arrow of
Deliverance, 1844.
PLATE 56B. H. P.
BRIGGS. First con-
ference   between
the Spaniards and
Peruvians,   1531,
1826.

B

PLATE 57A. SIR DAVID WILKIE. Study for Mary Queen of Scots escaping from Loch Leven, 1837.

PLATE 57B. R. B. MARTINEAU. Picciola, 1853.

PLATE 58A. SIR JOHN MILLAIS. The disentombment of Queen Matilda, 1849.

PLATE 58B. SIR DAVID WILKIE. Mehemet
Ali, wash drawing, 1841.

PLATE 59. D. G. ROSSETTI. Pencil drawing of Elizabeth Siddal,
c. 1860.

PLATE 60A. JOHN PARTRIDGE.
Sir Charles Eastlake. *c.* 1825.

PLATE 60B. WILLIAM ETTY. Hero and Leander, 1829.

PLATE 61A.
SIR CHARLES EASTLAKE.
Mrs Bellenden Kerr, 1835.

PLATE 61B. E. M. WARD. Lord Lytton in his Study, 1851.

PLATE 62A. JOHN E. CAREW.
Henry Wyndham, 1831.

PLATE 62B. JOHN GIBSON.
Queen Victoria, 1848.

PLATE 63A. WILLIAM BEHNES.
Prince George of Cumberland, 1828.

PLATE 63B. THOMAS WOOLNER.
Alfred, Lord Tennyson, 1857.

PLATE 64A. WILLIAM THEED THE YOUNGER. Narcissus, *c.* 1847.

PLATE 64B. JOHN E. CAREW. Adonis and the Boar, 1826.

PLATE 64C. JOSEPH DURHAM. Waiting his innings, 1866.